BOOKS BY THE SAME AUTHOR

The Freedom of Life
The Path of Life
The Helper of Men and Nature

The Christ We Know

THE CHRIST WE KNOW

SON OF MAN AND SON OF GOD:
MASTER, LORD AND SAVIOUR

BY THE RIGHT REVEREND
CHARLES FISKE, D.D., L.H.D., LL.D.
BISHOP OF CENTRAL NEW YORK

NEW YORK *and* LONDON
Harper & Brothers Publishers

TO MY WIFE

APOLOGIA

PREFACE TO NEW EDITION

*T*HIS book makes no pretension of being a new *Life of Christ*. It is an interpretation, a swift survey, written for those who could hardly undertake a more exacting study. It tries frankly to face some modern doubts and difficulties, questions raised by the latest biblical criticism, the problem of miracles, especially such difficulties as arise out of the story of the miraculous birth of Christ and his resurrection; but it endeavors to deal with such questions, not in terms of dogmatic theology, but simply and practically as they affect the attitude of the average person towards the traditional faith.

Above all else, the book tries to picture Christ in the winsomeness and attractiveness of his complete humanity and to show how the early disciples, out of their experience with their Master, moved slowly but surely to belief in him as a Divine Person. A letter which came to me after the book had passed through its first printing has pleased me beyond words. It says: "I like the book because it seems to have been written *con amore* and is therefore so lovable in its picture of the Christ who stilled into wonder the hearts of his first friends." Indeed, that is what I have most wanted to do; it has been in mind as the purpose of every sentence I have written— to make men see "the light of the knowledge of the glory of God in the face of Jesus Christ."

That there is special need of such a book is evident

from a letter recently received from a college pastor. "I want a book on the life of Christ," he writes, "which can be read by the average thoughtful person who really wishes to understand Christianity. Students come here from educated homes who show themselves amazingly ignorant of the simplest facts of the Christian religion and apparently possess not the slightest acquaintance with the life and teaching of its Founder. Later they often show a real interest in religion. Once they begin to think, I should like to lead them to a fuller knowledge of Christ. But they will not read such books about him as are in my library. There are two-volume biographies, rich in rabbinical lore. There are critical studies, with long dissertations on the sources of the gospel narratives. There are scholarly treatises, touching upon many questions of interpretation, invaluable to a pastor or preacher. There are deep theological studies; even philosophical studies of Christ. There are devotional biographies. There are books which picture Christ as an Oriental mystic; others which make him a socialistic radical; others, so obsessed with eschatology that they would have us believe he was a first century 'Adventist'; some which commend him as a glorified, spiritually minded member of a noonday luncheon club, the ideal of the modern business man; some which write of him with evangelical fervor, but expand the narrative beyond reasonable bounds by making every incident an occasion for pious meditation and adding pages upon pages of moralizing after the accepted homiletical manner. What we need is a book about Jesus Christ that will not attempt to tell the whole story, but will give the essential facts without too many confusing details. As for myself, I think we need some such short study to show the many-sided character of Jesus Christ and present him as his church has always believed in him—the God-man, who is Master, Saviour and Lord."

Such is the book I have tried to write—trying because I also know these young men and women of whom the college pastor speaks. Knowing them and many others like them, I want to introduce them to the real Jesus Christ whom I love and serve and in whom I believe with all my heart.

I have faith that they, too, would give love and service, if only they could be made to see him as he was seen by those who lived with him on earth, and capitulated when they came under his spell, and has been seen since by others, of every type of mind, and in every variety of circumstance, in all the days since he lived in Palestine. Would that his portrait could really be painted. Just the picture itself, the mere telling of the story of his life —without exhortation or appeal—is alluring. If rightly told, the story is absorbingly interesting. It is its own argument for the validity of our faith and its own proof of the possibilities of the life Christ offers abundantly.

Youth needs such a knowledge of Christ and of the real values of life as he estimated them. The present generation has full knowledge of the physical and material realm; what it lacks is knowledge of the moral and spiritual. It is ever demanding liberty of self-expression; but if self-expression be only in the realm of the physical, tragedy follows, "the lust of the flesh, and the lust of the eyes, and the pride of life"—or, as we should say, the pleasures of the senses, sensual enjoyment, sex obsessions, money madness, class ambitions, privileges, hatreds; against which repeated reproach has been thundered, all to no effect. Rebellious youth, in particular, has been urged to reform, in the name of custom, authority, tradition, only to answer with amusement or scorn of moral conventions and social taboos. If we can show that self-expression must be the expression of the *whole* self; that we need to set free the higher creative powers, that conscience and the finer instincts must not be neglected, that here lie the deepest satisfactions and the greatest happiness of life—then we have a real call; a summons to control the lower and lesser in order to give free play to the higher. Jesus Christ is the supreme revelation of God, but he is also the full expression of the best possibilities in human life. This book is written in the hope that it may make clear the beauty and attractiveness and power of the life he offers.

Meanwhile, if this is not exactly the book my college friend asked for, no one else has written it, and some one ought to try. This effort may encourage a better qualified man to supply the need. At least, the attempt to make others see the Christ I know has made me see him more clearly myself.

C. F.

Bishopstead
UTICA, NEW YORK

CONTENTS

CONTENTS

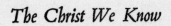

The Christ We Know

Chapter I: The Meaning of the Story

NINETEEN centuries ago there appeared in Palestine a great spiritual leader, Jesus, afterward known as the Christ, or Messiah, whose teachings have revolutionized the world's moral standards and influenced forever its conceptions of God and its estimates of life.

He taught, as no man had ever taught before, the things of God. He gave himself unselfishly to the service of men. He was true man in all that is essentially human. Yet those who were nearest to him gradually came to believe that he was more than man. By the beauty of his life and teaching, the wonder of his works, his miracles of love; by his unswerving devotion to truth and right; by the dynamic influence of his personality; finally, by what his followers believed to be his triumphant victory over death—Jesus was proclaimed as God.

He transformed the character of his adherents and in the power of his spirit they went into the world proclaiming a message that, when freely accepted, transformed others. Weak men showed moral strength and purpose. Untaught peasants gave evidence of unexampled spiritual insight. Their enthusiasm won adherence from the more enlightened. Numerous officials of the Jewish hierarchy accepted the new religion. Eventually leaders of the political and social life of the empire were brought to allegiance. Of course they were not always consistent or loyal to the truth they had accepted. Indeed, the world has done almost everything with the truth of Christianity except to hold firm in the practice of it. Yet eventually Christianity became the religion of the world and the name Christian, first given to the followers of Jesus in amused contempt, afterward became a title of honor. Christ has rarely failed to receive reverence, whatever men have thought of some who bear his name or of the churches that have claimed to represent him.

The story of Jesus Christ may begin with his birth and boyhood days, or with the opening of his public ministry, or with the first preaching of his gospel—the good news of God. Two of the four accounts written by the early biographers begin with the nativity, one starts with his public appearance as a teacher, one is an interpretive account of his life and work and opens with what we would call an estimate of his character.

This last is called the Gospel according to St.

John. For many years it has been the subject of severe critical study. More recently the sanest literary criticism has shown a tendency to go back to the traditional view of the authorship of the Gospel and attribute the work at least to one of the "school" of which St. John was the revered master. The opening words of the book fall with measured weight, slow, sure, steady, serious, and solemn. There is in them a breathless devotion and reverent sense of mystery. They speak of Jesus as the "Word of God," one who reveals the life of God as the written or spoken word expresses the thought of men. This prologue reads as follows:

"In the beginning was the Word, and the Word was with God, and the Word was God. The same was in the beginning with God. All things came into being through him, and apart from him was not anything made. That which was made in him was life. The life was the light of men. The light shineth in the darkness and the darkness overcame it not. There was the true light which lighteth every man coming into the world. He was in the world and the world knew him not. He came unto his own home and his own people received him not. But as many as received him, to them gave he the right to become children of God, even to them who believe on his name, who were born, not of bloods, nor of the will of the flesh, nor of the will of man, but of God. And the Word became flesh and tabernacled among us (and we beheld his glory—glory as of an only begotten from a Father) full of grace and truth."

That same sense of hushed devotion is felt in other words of the early followers of Christ. There is something poignantly beautiful in the language of St. Paul, who declared that he had seen "the light of the knowledge of the glory of God in the face of Jesus Christ." There is the same gladness of surprise in the words of one of the early apostolic letters (or epistles) in which the writer says: "That which was from the beginning, which we have heard, which we have seen with our eyes, which we have looked upon, and our hands have handled of the Word of Life; (for the life was manifested, and we have seen it and bear witness, and show unto you that eternal life, which was with the Father and was manifested unto us); that which we have seen and heard declare we unto you."

Again, when the aged Apostle Paul writes to his friend and pupil, Timothy, he reminds him how "great is the mystery of godliness"; how God was manifested in the flesh, proved just and holy through the spirit, and then (rising to phrases whose meaning has never been fully explained) adds that the God thus manifested in human life was "seen of angels, preached to the non-Jewish peoples, believed on in the world, received up into glory."

The world today is impatient of doctrine. Small wonder, when we remember that doctrine has nearly always been presented in hard, concentrated, dogmatic statements, with all too slight interest in its moral significance. That is not the way in which these first followers of Jesus Christ taught his divinity. Often their doctrinal statements are pressed solely to illustrate and enforce a moral truth. St. Paul pleads for his converts that the same mind may be in them which was also in Christ Jesus. One can almost see the look of awe in his eyes as he adds: "Being originally in the very form of God and of his nature, he did not think of this equality with God as a prize to be grasped and held fast, but emptied himself and took upon himself the form of a slave, and was made in the likeness of men, and became obedient unto death; more than that, the disgraceful death of a criminal on the cross." Indeed, one need not call upon the imagination in order to realize the solemn mystery of the words, for at once the Apostle goes on to tell how at the name of Jesus every knee bows in adoration, while all tongues proclaim his glory and call him Lord. He was, to use the words of another writer, "the brightness of the Father's glory and the express image (or stamped copy) of his person."

We cannot understand how the first preaching of Christianity proved so wonderfully effective, unless we realize that the early disciples lived in the warmth and glow of an experience the thrill of which never left them. We need to remind ourselves (whether we have fully accepted their view or not) that these men, to whom we go to gain our first impressions of Jesus Christ, lived in an atmosphere of reverence, devotion, amazement, and awe. They felt something of holy fear as they looked back at their friendship with their Friend and Master. Their remembrance of those days of friendly intercourse did not make them feel "chummy with the Almighty," to use a phrase which expresses the chief characteristic of some evangelistic preachers of today. They never went about the business of religion with breezy familiarity. They could not be familiar, of course, because they had a sense of the mystery, the beauty, and the glory of the experience they were trying to pass on the others. They lived as men who suddenly found themselves transplanted into another world. They felt that they had been in vivid contact with the divine. It so showed itself in their speech that others also felt the glory of it. Looking back to the days when the Lord Jesus had companied with them, they seemed to say: "Now—now, at last, we understand what it all meant."

What did it mean? Nothing less than this: that when they listened to his words they were hearing one who spoke, and had a right to speak, as the Voice of God; when they looked at him they were seeing God; when they touched him (wonder of wonders) they had actually touched God. They had gazed upon and their unworthy hands had handled the Word of Life.

It is this teaching of the early disciples of Christ which the ancient creeds of Christianity seek to express in compact language. When a child is born, a new person comes into the world. Whether they were right or wrong, it is apparent that the first Christians believed that when Jesus Christ was born, no new person entered into life here. It was the same divine Person who had lived through eternity with the Father and now took a new nature and in it manifested his eternal truth and beauty. "No man has seen God at any time; the only-begotten Son, who is in the bosom of the Father, has declared him"— make him known.

One cannot lightly dismiss this interpretation

of the life of Christ. It grips the imagination. Impossible? But how could it have been invented? What are often alleged to be similar ideas about the pagan gods, turn out, on examination, to be wholly unlike the Christian idea. Too good to be true? No; too splendid not to be true. It moves us to the heart. We cannot fail to be stirred to reverence and devotion if we will but lay aside, as far as possible, prejudices and presuppositions, and immerse our minds in the story itself. A poem by Browning tells of an Arab physician, Karshish, who writes a letter in which he describes meeting one Lazarus, who claimed to have been raised from the grave and believed that the one who brought him back to life was truly God. Karshish at first dismisses the tale with amused incredulity; but somehow the idea will not down. Soon he speaks of it again, as an unbelievable delusion, of course, but a story worth repeating. Then, the letter ended, he comes back to the tale, in a postscript, as it were; he plays about the thought with a strange fascination; he cannot dismiss it from his mind. Suppose it were true! "The very God! think, Ahib; so the All-Great were the All-Loving, too."

Nor is this view of the meaning of Christ's life a late interpretation. Certainly it is the view of St. Paul, and the authenticity of the principal writings of this apostle is now beyond controversy. Indeed, the tendency of modern criticism is to accept the Pauline epistles as "a proved guarantee for the historicity of the gospel story." Those epistles which are no longer open to question as the work of St. Paul are of earlier date than the four Gospels. They give us the first-hand witness of one who knew personally Peter and James and the other apostles and declared that what he taught he had "received" from them. They state with all possible clarity what the men who were closest to Jesus came to believe about him.

Chapter II: The Early Days

NO LOVELIER story has ever been told than the story of Christ's birth. Poetry and art have given of their best to tell the tale for each succeeding age. They can add little to the brief, beautiful accounts given in the gospels.

We are indebted to St. Matthew and St. Luke for the traditional account of the Christmas birth. St. Luke tells it as the mother of Jesus would have recorded her experiences. St. Matthew gives the account of the foster father.

The story begins with a scene in the Jewish temple, where Zacharias, an aged priest, was ministering, chosen by lot that day for the most honorable part of the service, the offering of incense in the holy place. He is childless and his wife is now beyond the age when children may be expected; but as he ministers before the altar he has a vision of an angelic visitor, who tells him that Elizabeth, his wife, will bear him a son. He cannot believe the promise and paralysis takes away his speech. It returns only when the prophecy is fulfilled and a child is born to whom he gives the name of John—that John who afterward appeared beyond the Jordan as the Baptizer and announced the coming of the Christ.

Then we turn to another scene, one of the most exquisitely beautiful that has ever been painted. We see a lovely Jewish maiden—Mary of Nazareth. To her also appears a heavenly visitant. As in the heart of every other Jewish woman, hope sang in her heart that some day she might be the mother of the Lord's anointed representative, the Messiah-King who would come to restore again its old place and power to the Jewish nation, and to strengthen and inspire it to fulfill what every devout Hebrew felt to be its great mission—to make the true God known to the world and to bring the nations to worship him in unity and peace.

The angel tells Mary that she has found favor with God and that he has chosen her for this high and holy task. Mary cannot understand. She is betrothed—not yet married—and the angel declares that the child will soon be hers. Unlike Zacharias, she believes, though she cannot understand; therefore to her comes the explanation. The Spirit of God shall rest upon her; the power of the Highest shall overshadow her; the child is to have no earthly father; "the holy thing" to be born of her shall be called, therefore, the Son of God.

Grant for a moment that the story is true, and never woman spoke a nobler or braver word than Mary's, when she said, "Be it unto me according to thy word." She gave her consent, with all that it meant of suspicion, misunderstanding, gossip, suffering—anguish so great that "a sword pierced her heart." After giving her consent, she is said to have spoken in words that are a poem and a song, rich in remembrance of the recorded history of another woman of older times, Hannah, who also had been blessed in a wonderful son, phrased in language reminiscent of the scripture story with which she was familiar.

Then the story turns to Joseph, to whom Mary was betrothed; tradition says a widower, much older than she. We need not do more than tell enough of him to do full justice to one whom history has hardly appreciated and to whom the Christian churches have never given sufficient reverence. He hears of Mary's condition, and thinking of her beauty, her virtues, her present danger, he is sick at heart as he carries his problem to God in prayer. Then he, too, has his vision, with the assurance of the divine origin of the child soon to be born; and he takes Mary at once to his home, where in the shelter of his love gossip can for a while forget her. It was the chivalrous act of a chivalrous man who had the simple faith and the robust honor of a true gentleman. And

Joseph had not only his vision, but his special message from God. To him came, first, the knowledge of what his foster son would do and by what name, therefore, he should be called: "Thou shalt call his name Jesus, for he shall save his people from their sins." To Mary is given a revelation of the greatness of her son, to Joseph the first word about his work.

"Jesus" the child was called, then, when the eight days were past after his birth and his name day arrived. It is the old Hebrew name Joshua —or "Jehovah (Jah) our Saviour." There were many men in Palestine who bore the same cognomen. Of the crowds who knew the Christ afterward as Jesus of Nazareth, few supposed that in his name there was any greater significance than in the names of the Simons and Judahs and Jameses around him.

Emphasis has been laid upon the divine nature of the Lord Jesus, but we shall see later that it is as much "heresy" to forget his actual, genuine and complete humanity as his real and full divinity. He was Son of Man—true son among the sons of men, having our human joys and sorrows, all the ordinary wants of human nature, the usual hungers of the human heart. His life covered but a narrow part of human experience, and we shall learn that this calls for special thought about his human example as a guide to his followers, but he was true man and can come closer to his brother men than any other companion.

Very little is told of Jesus until he began his work at the age of thirty. There are a few beautiful stories of his birth and infancy: the pilgrimage to Bethlehem, where Joseph and Mary journeyed to be enrolled in the census; the rest in the stable cave; the manger cradle; how the child was born in the stable where they had found lodgment when the mother's hour drew near, because the crowds that had come up for the enrolling filled the little town so that there was found "no room for them in the inn"; the contrast of humility and glory; the lowly birth and the divine majesty of the newborn child; the song the shepherds heard, when an angel voice announced, "Behold, I bring you good tidings of great joy which shall be to all people, for unto you is born this day in the city of David a Saviour, who is Christ the Lord"; and the glory that "shone round about them," while a chorus of other angelic voices sang, "Glory to God in the highest; and on earth, peace among men of good will"; the visit of the shepherds to the mother and child.

Later, doubtless, lodging was found elsewhere in the village. After eight days the child received his name "Jesus," and when forty days had passed, he was presented in the temple, a first-born child to be specially dedicated to God, with the accustomed sacrifice (in this case the offering of the poor), and then given back to the parents to be cared for as the returned "gift of God." It was in connection with this service that the aged Simeon and Anna, devout worshippers in the temple who "waited for the consolation of Israel," told of the mission of the child; and Simeon blessed them and spoke to Mary his mother of the sword that should pierce her heart and of how the child was "set for the fall and rising again of many in Israel and for a sign that shall be spoken against."

Later came the pilgrimage of the Eastern magi, who saw a star which told them of the birth of a King to the Jews. It will be remembered how, centuries after, Kepler, the astronomer, noticed a conjunction of Jupiter, Saturn and Mars in the Constellation of the Fishes, with a brilliant star near them. Some have thought that it was this star that led the astrologers to look for the King. Then followed their visit, their gifts; the jealous rage of Herod; the martyrdom of the innocent children of Bethlehem; the flight of the mother and the foster father to Egypt with the child; the home-coming to Nazareth; the first visit of the boy to Jerusalem; the impression he made upon the temple teachers; his life of filial obedience and subordination at home; the early departure of his cousin John to become a wilderness hermit; his own thirty years of preparation before the clear call came to take up his life work.

Controversy has always raged about the nativity story and always will. Let it be stated, at once, that belief in this miraculous birth and acceptance of the deity of Christ are two separate and distinct matters of faith. One cannot suppose that the story of the birth ever became known to the apostles until long after their faith in Christ had become fixed. Of course it was not generally told. One can readily see why it would not have been told by Jesus himself. It is obvious that it could not have been made generally known during the lifetime of his mother. It ought to be equally clear that it could never be pleaded as a reason for accepting the faith in Christ as the unique Son of God. That had to rest, so a great scholar has reminded us, on public events to which the apostles could bear witness within their own experience.

We may go further and say that one cannot quite imagine the fact of a miraculous birth being told to the apostles until after their own faith was established, any more than one can imagine Jesus abruptly announcing to them his godhead. It was of the very essence of his method that the apostles should come slowly to their understanding of him. He could not "tell them plainly" who he was; they had to learn for themselves. Had the knowledge been thrust upon them, instead of gradually "sliding into their minds," the naturalness of their life with him would have been lost and one purpose of his coming defeated, in that they could never have had intimate fellowship with him. It was not until after the resurrection that the full meaning of his life broke upon them. One can quite see, however, that after they had learned the mystery of Christ's nature, then the beautiful story of his birth came to them to help them to fuller understanding. While belief in Christ's deity is not based upon belief in a miraculous birth, the two are so congruous that the coming of the Divine Son can hardly be thought of as taking place in any other way.

The account of the virgin birth may, therefore, be accepted without difficulty by one who has first accepted the traditional faith of Christianity in the divine lordship of its founder. One cannot, on merely critical grounds, reject the nativity stories. And most people love them, and will not let them go, unless in all honesty they feel that they must. The wondering mother, the singing angels, the worshipping shepherds, the mysterious Magi—if we must drop them out, at least let us have enough reverence to go about the task without thoughtless haste and loud declamation. There are people who are already sufficiently disturbed, confused and grieved by the threatened loss of what they hold dear, without doubling their anguish through the flippancy of others who rush into print with all their doubts at the slightest provocation.

One suggestion surely has weight in our approach to the problem. In other ways, and by very different experiences, the apostles came to their faith in Christ as divine. They believed in him as a person already eternally existing and *afterward* taking to himself our human nature, not a new human personality—a divine person living a human life, that he might reveal in it what God's life is, and translate God's thought into our language.

You may not believe that Christ's coming means all that, though it will be worth while to read on and see, if you may, the reasons for such faith; but for those who do so believe—and many who deny the miraculous birth declare that this is their faith—it is hard to see why they should balk at one more bit of miracle. If Christ was not a "deified" man, but God manifested in human nature, it becomes evident at once that his birth was a miracle, whether he was born of a virgin or was not.

Moreover, the Gospel accounts of the virgin birth would never have been questioned, were it not that modern teachers are anxious to eliminate the supernatural from the Christian religion. They cannot do it and have much of the Christian religion left. People find it hard to accept the story of the nativity miracle, because they find it almost impossible to accept miracles, and they think they can have Christ's life and teaching without them. We shall consider, later, the question of miracles. For the present, it is enough to say that they are of the very warp and woof of the gospel story. When we try to eliminate them entirely, there is very little of a life story left.

Some who do not (or declare that they do not) stumble at miracles have an instinctive disaffection for the story of the virgin birth because it seems to them to rise out of a distorted view of married life and sex relationships. They forget that the ages which gladly believed the story are the ages which had high ideals of family life.

Is it not a fact that the story fits, with most extraordinary congruity, into the whole drama of the incarnation? God was making a new start for the human race. In nothing was there—in nothing is there still—such desperate need of a new beginning as in the matter of sex. The instinct of earlier days, which accepted the story in childlike faith and found in it childlike delight, is a right instinct; certainly, it is not lightly to be disregarded.

Chapter III: How Belief Began

ELIEF in Christ is not dependent upon the story of his miraculous birth. The apostles probably came to their faith long before they had ever heard the story. How, then, did their belief grow?

It began in one of the richest of all human experiences, an intimate friendship. Jesus Christ chose a few men for close companionship, training them until they were able to understand the meaning of his life and then sending them into the world to bring God to men in the glory of a new discovery.

The story of the life of the Twelve and their Master is full of charm. He walked with them through the fields and hills of Galilee, slept with them under the evening stars, talked with them in the intimacy of friendly companionship. His speech was of the simple things of their daily life. He talked of the woods and the winds and the weather, of the farmer sowing seed in the field, of the growing grain, of the fields whitening to harvest, of the women grinding grain at the mill, of the housewife kneading bread, of the bride and the piece of silver she had lost from her wedding necklace, of the guests at a wedding feast, of the master and manager of a great estate, of the shepherd and the lost sheep, of the dealer in precious stones and the pearl for which he risked his whole capital, of fishermen at their nets, of children playing in the public square, of the reckless and impatient boy who left home to try out his talents in the world; talked of these everyday things of life, until they saw all life in a spiritual light and every common bush seemed afire with God; talked of the God whom Hebrew theology had made remote and unapproachable and Hebrew religious rites had lost in a maze of religious machinery; talked of a spiritual world back of the material universe, until God became very real and very near.

These friends of Jesus Christ first met him beyond the Jordan, where John was preaching, quickening hundreds into penitent confession, and baptizing his converts in the river.

The history of the Hebrew people shows a gradual growth in their idea of God. First they believed in Him, apparently, as hardly more than a tribal deity. Then He became the one God, holding all nations in His care. Then they saw that He was, not merely the creator, but the moral governor of the universe. Later He be-

came "a god with a character," the High and
Holy One that inhabiteth eternity; holy Himself
and demanding moral character in His people.
Then they thought of Him as God of love and
mercy. Finally Jesus revealed Him as Friend
and Father.

Most of the moral difficulties of the Old Testament cease to trouble us, if we remember that it
records an evolution in morality and that the
knowledge of God develops only as men are made
ready for new ideas of His power and goodness.
Many of the other problems of the Old Testament are cleared up, if we remember also that
it is primarily a book of manners and morals and
a guide to faith. It is not an inspired manual of
science, nor is it a divinely dictated handbook
of history. Its writers are dependent upon the
knowledge of their own day. They gather many
myths and legends, current in many nations, but
to a very remarkable degree they succeed in purg·
ing these of what is gross and evil, telling them
anew with clear moral purpose.

The essence and core of the Old Testament
teaching is found in the writings of the prophets.
They were not primarily foretellers, clearly and
unequivocally announcing future events; they were
rather forth tellers, men of singular moral dis-
cernment, able to read the signs of the times and
declaring what would follow as the inevitable re-

sults of the social and political conditions of their day, statesmen, some of them, who struggled bravely to keep the nation true to what they believed to be Israel's destined duty in making God known to the world. A succession of prophetic voices led the nation on to new and better thoughts of God and interpreted history to show how He was "working His purpose out as age succeeded age." Despite much that is difficult to explain in the age-long evolution in the idea of God, it is even more difficult to explain in any ordinary way the clear teaching of this succession of prophets, from the rustic herdsman to the cultured courtier, each adding something new to the divine conception and, by comparison with the life and thought of other nations, something so strikingly true and original as to suggest more than natural insight.

For centuries now there had been no recognized prophetic voice in Israel. Then John appeared beyond the Jordan. He was a young man, wind-beaten and weather-browned from the wilderness life, clothed in rough yellow garments of camel's-hair cloth, carrying a pilgrim's staff and wearing a pilgrim's girdle, with a look in his eyes and a tone in his voice which made men feel that he had lived near to God.

John talked of serious things in a serious way.

All sorts of people flocked to hear him—plain members of the "proletariat" who listened to him as a social reformer; other men whose hearts he aroused to a sense of their own unworthiness; officials of the ruling class; ecclesiastics who listened, curious, anxious, suspicious, doubtful; a few quiet, earnest folk who mourned over the moral decline of the nation and found in John's preaching hope for the coming of the Messiah-King who would restore again the kingdom to Israel.

At last the crowds became so great and the excitement so intense that the ecclesiastical authorities began an investigation. They sent a delegation to the Jordan to question John. Just what were they to expect of him? What were his claims? Who was he? Why was he baptizing? What was the meaning of the new movement? Was he the Messiah? Honest, loyal, truthful, faithful witness that he was, he said, "No." Was he the prophet like Moses whom they all expected to appear some day? "No." Was he Elijah returned in the flesh? "No," again.

"What then," they asked; "who are you?" And he answered: "What difference does it make who I am? It is not myself that matters; it is my message. I am just a voice; a voice crying, 'In the wilderness prepare ye the way of the Lord; in the desert make straight a highway for our God.' Never mind about me. I am only the herald of another. The Messiah is coming and that is what concerns you; for you must make a way for him to come to your hearts and enter into your lives. That is the reason I baptize. It is a symbolic cleansing. One is coming after me who in honor is preferred before me. He is so great that I am not worthy to stoop down and unlace his sandals. Never mind me; listen to my message. Is that true or is it not true? Do you need to repent or do you not? If you neglect this baptism of repentance, there will come soon an unsparing baptism of fire, a judgment day of God when He will separate the wheat and the chaff and burn the chaff as hopelessly worthless."

A new kind of revival preacher, indeed; not much in him to remind one of the revivalists of modern times, who think a great deal of what people say about them, are only too anxious to secure a personal following, and love to drink of the waters of public adulation!

So Jerusalem and the nation felt the excitement. The Messianic idea was in the air. In the temple, in the synagogues, in court circles, and in the market place, everyone waited in anticipation. Even the rough Roman soldiers who came to the Jordan to look on with curiosity or to scoff remained to pray. All asked questions and all received plain, straight answers.

Among the earnest few who responded to the call to repentance were two men, Andrew and (probably) John, son of Zebedee, who afterward became followers of Jesus. One day they were standing with their master, John, when he pointed to a man on the edge of the crowd, a quiet, dignified figure in the white robe of a traveling rabbi, and cried out: "Look! There he is, the one who is in honor before me. Look! The Lamb of God who takes away the sin of the world."

The next day he pointed again to the traveling teacher. It was Jesus, his own relative, and he told how Jesus also had come for baptism; how John had refused to receive him for the rite, feeling instinctively his goodness; how Jesus had insisted on identifying himself with the repentant people, and how at the baptism a strange thing had happened—a dove, or something like one in its swift flight, had alighted on Jesus' head, and a voice declared his divine mission.

The two disciples who heard John speak followed Jesus, though when he turned to ask them what they desired they could only stammer an embarrassed request to know where he was sojourning. He invited them to come with him and they stayed all the rest of the day. Years afterward the writer of the story remembered the very hour when they met him. It was ten o'clock in

the morning. This was their introduction to
Jesus.

The following days were full of interest. Andrew brought his brother Simon and introduced
him to Jesus; probably John brought his brother
James. Christ found Philip and Philip brought
Nathanael, also called Bartholomew. Later there
were added six others to the intimate circle of
friends: Matthew, who was a collector of customs; Simon the Zealot, a radical; Thomas, a
plain, common-sense, matter-of-fact man, who
found it hard to accept what he could not understand, but had extraordinary loyalty; another
James, about whom traditional accounts vary;
Judas, the brother of James, also called Thad-
daeus; and Judas Iscariot, who became the betrayer of his Master—called Iscariot because he
was a man of Kerioth.

It must not be supposed that these were called
at once to apostleship and immediately left their
work and followed. There seems to have been a
growth in their friendship with Christ which led
to the later choice. At first, they were merely
friends; then they, with others, became "disciples," that is, pupils and learners, possibly on the
same footing as some seventy others who were
sent out on evangelistic journeys; at length, after

spending a whole night in prayer, Jesus selected these dozen men for chief office in his work. When they were chosen, therefore, they were ready to answer the call. Indeed, it would not have been natural or right for them to leave everything and follow him until they had been so prepared and until he knew their capacity for loyalty and leadership.

It seems to have been the purpose of Christ to make these men officers and ministers of the church he meant to establish. He gave them a distinctive title, "apostles," or men sent on a mission; the general name of "disciple," or pupil, was given to all, the apostles included. As the years of his public ministry drew to a close, he retired more and more from the crowds that always followed him, apparently put aside opportunities of service, sought privacy more frequently, took quiet journeys with this small group of friends, trained them with painstaking care, bent all his energies toward making them understand the secret of his life, and finally declared that upon the rock of their faith he would build his church.

This, then, was the beginning of their faith in Jesus. To them he was the Christ, or Messiah.

Through many centuries, as Israel proved more

and more a disappointment and a failure in carrying to other nations the knowledge of God, there had grown up belief in this Messiah-King who was to come as God's special representative, restore the kingdom, regenerate its people, give them real moral leadership in world affairs, awaken again the "God-consciousness" that had made them, more than other people, vehicles of an enlarging revelation, and quicken them to a new responsibility in spreading the truth with which they had been entrusted.

The real failure of the Jews was their inability to understand what it meant to be a "chosen people." Instead of realizing that their blessings were to be shared with others, they rested in complacent pride in their special calling. They were "one hundred per cent" Hebrews. Like Americans who cannot understand any type of people other than themselves, or realize that the opportunities they enjoy bring special responsibility, so these Jews became a self-satisfied nation, contemptuous of the "dogs of the Gentiles," forgetful that blessings and privileges are given to be shared, not to be hugged to one's own heart.

Among the Lord's disciples were patriots of deeper devotion, who hoped and prayed for a time when Israel would be restored to power and would use its influence and gifts for the world's good. The preaching of John the Baptist had brought them, in penitent acknowledgement of national faults and personal sins, to welcome the man he had pointed out as the Messiah. The first step in faith was their confident acceptance of Jesus as the Christ. Many of their ideas about his leadership were to be dispelled before their companionship with him was over; they were to learn that he would not "take his power and reign," that the Messiah was to be a "suffering servant," that the path to victory ran to Calvary and the cross. It is one of the wonders of their story that, with the exception of Judas the Betrayer, they held fast their faith in this Messiah, even though he dispelled almost all their ideas of his purpose and work. In considering their final belief, the strength of their faith is the more astounding, when we remember that it grew out of the failure of all their expectations. To find in a triumphant Messiah and King some special revelation of God might have been reasonable even for Jews who were trained in a severely monotheistic belief; but to find such a revelation in one who failed to win the nation, who antagonized its leaders, who discouraged their national ambitions, turned away from those who asked of him political leadership, and in the end aroused such bitter enmity that he was executed as a criminal—

that is faith which proves the worth of the men who declared it; faith which is so strong that we are not surprised to learn that it swept thousands into the church when in after days the work of winning men began.

Chapter IV: Christ's Example

HEN Jesus appeared at the Jordan and met his first followers, he came from the wilderness—the remote and lonely country where John had spent his years of preparation. Here, apparently, Jesus also spent forty days, or thereabouts, in facing his life work and mission and deciding on his future course.

Probably most of those who now read the story of the Temptation of Christ have the vaguest possible conception of its real significance. We have a mental image of those weeks of spiritual conflict that robs them of all human reality. Of course it is a dramatic recital, not a literal account. "Half the difficulties in the New Testament would vanish, if men would only consent not to translate Oriental poetry into bald, matter-of-fact, western prose." Our real difficulty, however, is to see how the story tallies with any experience of our own.

Perhaps we shall best understand, if we keep in mind the fact that Jesus had just come from his baptism, had been recognized by John as the

Messiah, and was soon to be publicly acknowledged by him. At his baptism he had received, in the mysterious voice from heaven, the assurance of his unique personality and power. That sense of the difference between himself and other men had always been with him, but now he had new evidence of it. There he stood, then, at the threshold of his life work and his Messianic mission. He was the destined reconciler of men to God, the founder of a new kingdom. Now the years of preparation for his work were over and it was time to begin.

It is no wonder that he sought the quiet wilderness. He had to be alone. He must have time to think, to formulate his plans; rather, to receive his Father's message and learn his Father's plan for him.

The threefold temptation, if we read the story with this in mind, is the record of the way in which he resisted all arguments for seeking some short cut to success. He could win his way by cultivating the crowd and riding into power on a wave of popularity. Or, he could look at his task as the world would view such service and think only of the influence he might gain and the kingdoms he might win. Meanwhile, he had great powers: would it not be perfectly lawful to use them to make his own task easier and his life more comfortable? Why not? Why suffer unnecessary handicaps? And why not be sensible and seek the easiest way of doing his work?

The same temptations recurred all through his life—when Peter sought to hold him back on the last journey to Jerusalem; when the Pharisees asked him for a sign; when the taunting watchers on Calvary told him that if he would come down from the cross they would believe. These are temptations such as come to every man who knows himself to be endowed with great gifts and understands that he should use them for God, yet feels himself constantly lured from the heights and asking whether he cannot seek an easier road and walk a smoother path.

Jesus was in the wilderness, therefore, by a kind of moral necessity. Resolutely putting into the background any thought of personal comfort, he bent himself to the task of translating the message he knew God would give him; he would think, and think hard, till he could be sure of God's purpose; think, and think hard, lest the spell of his recent experience pass away; concentrate on his task with purpose so intent as to transcend all ordinary interruptions and even make him oblivious of the need of sleep and food.

As the result, he saw clearly what sort of Messiah he must be; not the king the crowd expected —again and again he waved away such a crown; not one who would stoop to popular conceptions of Messiahship and modify his own convictions; a leader who would not use force even in a great crisis. He came out from the wilderness, sure that he must follow the path of truth and right, no matter where it led and no matter what it cost. God never meant to make life easy; he meant to make men great. God wants men of tremendous persistence and unflinching determination to live true to the best, men who will always do what truth and honor demand and close the ear against any suggestion of compromise with divine principles and purposes.

So Jesus came out of the wilderness, sure in his conception of the Messiah's office and work, certain in his thought of God's will for the Messiah's life, conscious that persistence in his purpose would lead to death, determined to make men see, nevertheless, that his way was God's way, and convinced that in the end the world would learn that he was right, and that sometime truth would win acceptance and prevail.

These considerations will suggest also how the example of Christ may be valid for us who live in a very different world from that of his day.

One who attends church with any frequency must sometimes wonder what the congregation is thinking about when the sermon time comes. Do they actually expect anything real, practical, vital?

Does the preacher touch their problems, enter into their thought, meet their difficulties; or is the sermon merely the conventional expression of conventionally correct sentiments, academically sound, idealistically beautiful, but never coming to grips with real life?

One feels it especially when the sermon attempts to set forth the example of Christ. How can we find in his life a real example? He lived in a simple age, while we live in a complex age, with all sorts of problems arising out of our complicated social, industrial and economic order. How can we find in Jesus an answer as to what position we should take, for example, in questions of capital and labor, of reasonable profits, of labor unions and their methods, of public ownership of public utilities, of women in industry, or the minimum wage? These are problems on which almost all of us feel obliged to come to some conclusions. If we desire to fix our attitude as one who seeks to follow the example of Jesus and walk in his steps, how is it possible? He never lived our life, we feel, nor met our special difficulties.

More than that, he lived a simple life, even for that simple age. He was a traveling teacher, going on pilgrimages from place to place, dependent upon chance hospitality. There was a reason for this; only in the freedom and intimacy of such a life, in such a day, could he have trained his apostles. But in our day, we cannot live such a life—unless we are ready to give up all modern conveniences, do away with business and government, pull down our modern cities, stop commerce and industry, and cast civilization into the discard.

What Jesus actually did was something finer than merely to give us an exact and precise model on which to pattern our lives. He wrote the law of life in the large. We study his life, and at once we discover certain principles which guided him—brotherliness, kindliness, friendliness; unselfish service; courageous adherence to truth and right; the God-ward uplift and outlook. Sometimes one wishes that one could be told exactly what to do in certain circumstances, but that is not Christ's way. Such a moral example would make life easier, perhaps, but it would make us human automatons. We need the discipline of thinking things out for ourselves. That is the only way our moral insight can become keen. It is the only way that makes for moral growth. It leads to enrichment of life. It brings spiritual strength as the sense of obligation grows.

If we could read the story of Christ with eyes open to this view of his human example, it would make us quick to understand the winsomeness and attractiveness of his character; perhaps it would

lead some earnest though misguided religionists
to a better understanding of the Christian life.
They have drifted into a wrong conception of
Christianity. It is not a negative and prohibitory
code, with a series of "Thou shalt nots." It does
not, therefore, call for the aggressive manage-
ment of other people's business, an intrusive reg-
ulation of their morals, or the attempted stand-
ardizing of their brains. American ecclesiastical
moralists have made religion dull, drab, gray and
overcast, whereas Jesus made it glowingly at-
tractive. He made morality, also, personal and
concrete, and therefore warm and appealing;
whereas before it had been abstract, admirable,
perhaps, but cold as ice. He brought back the
thrill to moral effort—a thrill which some suppose can be felt only in revolt.

We miss the whole force of Christ's example
if we try to follow literally in his steps, and we
commit a still worse error if we suppose that
we can get round the ensuing difficulty by setting
up disciplinary rules and regulations. There are
large sections of life in which the literal effort
to follow the example of Christ would be impossible. This forces us, not to the framing of rules,
but to the discovery of principles. We shall see,
soon, how this explains some of the teaching of
the Sermon on the Mount. Jesus never told men
precisely what they must do; he developed their

[39]

spiritual powers by forcing them to find out for themselves. He did not tell Zacchæus, the Jericho tax collector, to give away half his fortune, but by some means Zacchæus felt that he must do so. St. Paul, we may remember, did not directly counsel Philemon to give freedom to Onesimus, the runaway slave whom Paul was sending back with a letter to his rich friend; but Philemon could hardly have failed to recognize his duty as the slave's "brother in Christ Jesus."

This was always Christ's way. He wanted men to make their own discoveries and come to their own decisions. Even his divinity they learned by experience. They lived with him, found in him such an impression of love and power as stilled their hearts, discovered themselves acting toward him as they would toward God, realized that he permitted and encouraged this attitude—and finally were compelled to ask, "Why?"

Christian morality compels us, in like manner, always to voice our "why," always to question "how," always to go upon our own voyages of discovery and make our own ventures of faith. It is the way of growth. There is never a voice that cannot be stilled, never a command that cannot be misinterpreted. We find out for ourselves what is right and good as we measure life by Christ's laws. There are no set lines, no fixed prohibitions, no clearly defined duties, no clean-cut rules, yet the example is no less real, the moral compulsion no less great. It is so great that one who honestly tries to follow Christ's example soon discovers how high his standards are, and can hardly escape the questions which Jesus himself asked his followers, "What think ye of Christ?" "Who say ye that I am?"

Chapter V: The Great Teacher

HORTLY after the days at the Jordan, Jesus began his public ministry. He was not a preacher. One cannot easily think of him in the pulpit. Perhaps it would help religion if many pulpits were torn down and we had less preaching and more simple, direct, earnest, natural speech about spiritual things. Jesus never preached, in the modern sense of the word. He taught, and taught by gathering people about him for quiet, friendly speech.

In the early days of his ministry, he was the sensation of the hour. Crowds followed him; the common people heard him gladly. They had been accustomed to the dry-as-dust discourses of the ecclesiastical teachers, with their meticulous examination of laws and precedents and their careful exposition of rules of conduct and worship. His speech, by contrast, seemed like a breath of fresh air in a musty room.

The nearest approach to a sermon of which there is any record was a simple talk in his home synagogue, when he took a text from the scripture lesson of the day. This was the text: "The

Spirit of the Lord is upon me, because he hath anointed me to preach the good news to the poor; he hath sent me to heal the broken-hearted, to preach deliverance to the captives, and recovering of sight to the blind, to set at liberty them that are bruised, to preach the acceptable year of the Lord." When he closed the book, we are told that "the eyes of all that were in the synagogue were fastened on him," as he told them that "this day is this scripture fulfilled in your ears." At first they wondered at the gracious words that fell from his lips, and began to ask whether he were really the carpenter's son; but afterward his speech became more plain. Was a prophet without honor in his own country? Well, had it not always been so? How many of the chosen people in earlier days had missed a blessing which others outside the covenant nation had received!

This was not the way to please strict Jews! His first sermon in his home town filled the people with such rage that an attempt was made to kill him. The truth is, that from the beginning of his career as a teacher, he insisted on breaking down "the wall of partition" between Jew and Gentile and made his message one that met the needs of men of every race and class. He was more than a Hebrew Messiah; he was to be the World's Redeemer.

What is known as the Sermon on the Mount is perhaps a collection of his "talks on religion," or a more formal compend of his precepts. The full text of an address is found in St. Matthew's Gospel. Critics are now agreed that the narrative of the first gospel is built around a collection of Christ's utterances or "sayings." Thus we have gathered into one discourse a group of seven parables; in another section, there is combined a series of utterances about the judgment upon Jerusalem and the final judgment of the world; there is, again, a stern denunciation of the Pharisees which seems unquestionably to be a combination of several addresses recorded elsewhere. Probably, therefore, the Sermon on the Mount is a grouping of a body of teachings given at other times and probably often repeated in substance.

This does not mean that an address was not actually delivered to the company who gathered around Jesus on the hillside; at least part of it must have been given on that occasion, certainly, we may suppose, the early portion, with the Beatitudes. Nor does it follow, because some of the sermon is recorded in shorter form as delivered under other circumstances, that it may not have been expanded and repeated in substance on the hillside; indeed, it is likely that many of the Lord's sayings were repeated by him many times and in many ways. Probably, however, the editor of the first gospel sought to gather Christ's teachings into a formal compend, while St. Luke tried to place them in some consecutive order in a narrative which would supply their "setting."

At any rate, the Sermon on the Mount is clearly a coherent address, logical in its movement, setting forth the sum and substance of his teaching. It has been called "the new law." That gives, at once, a wrong impression of the way in which Christ taught. He does not lay down laws: he gives principles of conduct; he does not prescribe rules: he describes a character; he is interested in showing his followers what they must be, rather than what they must do.

How does he describe the character he would build up in his followers? The world has its own standards for estimating a man's worth and its own ideas of happiness and success. The teaching of Jesus cuts across these standards. Do you want to be happy, or blessed? Then, he says, learn that real happiness comes to the man who is willing, if need be, to be poor and is therefore detached from possessions. Real happiness, again, does not come by seeking all possible pleasures and shutting one's eyes to everything unpleasant or troublesome, declining to permit anything to make too large a draft upon one's emotions or sympathy; happy is the man who can enter into the world's sin and sympathize with its sorrow and suffering, until it hurts; blessed are they that mourn. Once more, the world regards as happy the man who has won his rights and holds all possible privileges and dignities; Christ declares that the man who thinks little of his rights and does not always stand on his dignity or seek to enforce his claims will in the end receive the larger heritage. There are many desires that most men long to have satisfied; the truly happy man is the one who is eager to enrich his inner life, who is literally hungry and thirsty for goodness. Many men think more of justice than of mercy and are fearful of betrayal into emotional reactions; true happiness comes to the man who lets himself go and is full to overflowing of kindness and forgiveness. Real peace, too, comes to the man who has singleness of heart; the knowledge of God is for the pure-minded. Class jealousies, race hatreds, fierce competition between individuals, again, break a man's peace of soul. The happiest man is he who is a peacemaker, bringing races and classes, neighbors and nations, rich and poor, hand workers and head workers, into reconciliation and better understanding. Yet peace must not be purchased at any price. Persecution for conviction may bring more of peace than of pain. The happiest man is the man who is so sure of his faith and so passionately devoted to truth, that "the slings and arrows of outrageous fortune" and the sting of misunderstanding can no longer disturb his peace of spirit.

The happy man whom Christ describes is like salt that gives savor, like light in a dark place. Character is the one thing no one can keep to himself. Goodness is a quality that is always being communicated.

In the rest of the address, Jesus goes on to revise and reinterpret the old law; to declare the real motive of the Christlike life; to show its chief characteristics. The official teachers of the law laid emphasis upon outward observances; he puts the emphasis on inner motives. They were content with obedience to statutory enactments and asked nothing better than a severely strict acquiescence in the ethical standards of the time; he asks a willingness to go over and beyond the most that men may demand. They were content to be a little better than most men; he asks for that "divine discontent" which strives for perfection. They obeyed rules and did the good that could be expected of them, in order that they might be respected by the community; he asks men to live in constant remembrance of God and with desire above all else to win His approval and blessing. This means that the followers of Jesus can never be unduly critical of others, will always show real considerateness, will, in fact, be magnanimous and generous, men of the large heart. The spirit of his teaching has best been summarized in the Golden Rule, which is not wholly new with himself and finds its real originality in its positiveness. Abstention from wrongdoing is not enough: we must be occupied in good. It is not sufficient to do no one any harm: we must have full and equal consideration for others, as we would expect thoughtfulness from them.

Three things should be noticed about our Lord's teaching in the Sermon on the Mount; first, the authority with which he teaches; second, the form in which the teaching is cast; third, the character of the teacher.

His authority. The old law which he revised was regarded as God-given. "It was said to them of old time." What a tremendous claim Christ makes, when he presumes to place himself on a level with the One who gave this law directly to Moses—for so it was believed that the law came. "It was said to them of old time (said by God Himself through His servant); but now *I* say to you." Even those who are strongest in their convictions can at the most declare such convictions: I believe; I feel sure; I am certain. Christ says, "I know"; and the *know* of his voice still rings through the ages.

The form of his teaching. He taught vividly, by paradox and epigram. If we take his words and try to turn them into humdrum legalities, they are absurd. "Give to him that asketh thee and from him that would borrow of thee turn not thou away"—that would put a premium on idleness and beggary. "Lay not up for yourselves treasures on earth"—as literal law, that would discourage thrift, condemn business and commerce, destroy the social order. "If a man sue thee at the law, and take away thy coat, let him have thy cloak also"—it would put the lawyers out of business, but it would also encourage lawlessness and give loose rein to injustice. "If a man smite thee on thy right cheek, turn to him the other also"—that would in most cases provoke further violence, rather than turn aside wrath. He himself did not turn the other cheek when the servants smote him at his trial in the high priest's house. His words were never dully literal.

Remember that the language is oriental, vivid, paradoxical, aphoristic, epigrammatic, and at once we see that we have no enunciation of legalistic commands: we have the setting forth of principles. In looking at the example of Christ, we see that he does not give precise, specific, definite laws of life. He leaves us to do something for ourselves. He would have us do some hard work in the way of character building. In each of his sayings there is a principle to be discovered and applied: to cultivate the spirit of abounding generosity; to control acquisitiveness; to show magnanimity and large-heartedness; to curb personal resentment. It is for us to discover the kernel of truth in the parable or paradox and apply it in the varying circumstances of life.

Is not that the way in which truth is often made vivid? We have paradoxical teaching in many of the proverbs of the wise among men, and we seldom misunderstand their meaning. "Look before you leap." Of course; it is a wise precaution. Yet, "Nothing venture, nothing have"; true again, of course, we cannot always be trembling on the anxious edge of decision. "A penny saved is a penny earned." To be sure; thrift is always praiseworthy—that is, unless it be meanness; we may become "penny wise, pound foolish." The ideal teacher is the one who makes you *see the idea,* not the one who loses the thought in a maze of detail, much less in a cautious catalogue of exceptions.

It is a splendid and inspiring task, in the world in which we live and with the tasks we have to do and the temptations we must overcome, to try to read "the mind of the Master" in the effort to discover what Jesus Christ would expect of us. Only a weakling would wish a map of duty, with all the directions plainly printed. Christ's call is to live unselfishly, to give gladly and generously, to break through the tyranny of class and reverse the usual order of life and think more of others than of self. It is our part to ask, "When?" and "Where?" and "Why?"

It is this that makes the teaching of Jesus universal. No new generation has improved upon it and no new civilization will supplant it. Conditions change and the application varies, but the principles abide. Every age has found its highest ideals embodied in Christ. He has been the perfect truth to ages of philosophic thought; the highest example to an age of discipline; the quickener of the dead letter to an age of ecclesiastical reform; the example of service to our own practical age; the awakener of conscience to a generation which faces the social problem; the hope of those who seek peace for the world.

His character. And, then, marvel of marvels: he *was* all that he taught. Will his teaching work? Look at him and we see that it *has* worked. Other teachers have had beautiful thoughts; the higher their ideals, the sharper the contrast with their actions and the more evident the difference between what men say and what they are. Jesus Christ has always been the living embodiment of every word of his teaching. Not only does he say, "I know"; he adds, "I am."

Chapter VI: The Friendly Road

ESUS himself lived a happy life. We forget this because his career ended in sacrifice and suffering. Christian theology has often made the Cross of Calvary the whole substance of its teaching. It was not always so. In earlier days the church was concerned with the thought of the incarnation—belief in the deity of the Lord, manifested in a perfect humanity. The first teachers could never forget that they had seen "the light of the knowledge of the glory of God in the face of Jesus Christ." In our own day— an age of practical activity, rather than of speculative thought—the emphasis is more often placed on the human example of Christ and the need of following him as "The Way" as well as "The Truth and the Life." He is

". . . . . the Christ of our hearts and homes,
Our hopes and prayers and needs,
The Brother of want and blame,
The Lover of women and men,
With a love that puts to shame
All passions of mortal ken."

[52]

For centuries both these aspects of the great life were almost forgotten in the exclusive insistence upon the sacrifice of Christ as an atonement for the sin of the world—an emphasis so jealous as to minimize other truths and shift the center of Christian teaching. This meant that Jesus was rarely thought of save as "a man of sorrows and acquainted with grief."

In Holman Hunt's picture, "The Shadow of the Cross," the youthful Jesus and his mother are seen together in the carpenter's shop at Nazareth. As the sun streams through the doorway, it casts upon the opposite wall in the form of a cross the shadow of his body and outstretched arms. Mary sees the shadow. In the agony of her posture there is suggested the idea that from his boyhood days the shadow of the cross always fell upon his path and darkened his life. There is truth, of course, in the picture—it is quite legitimate to let the imagination have play in reading thus early the significance of the later tragedy— but there is error also; the exaggerated emphasis which not only makes the cross the center of Christian teaching, but can hardly see anything in Christianity except the cross. We need not feel that the only purpose of Christ's coming was that he might die for men. Nor is it natural to think of his cross as if such an end to his career were so inevitable that he himself apparently had no real choice about it.

That is not true. However dark the latter days, the early years of his ministry were full of joy, gay and light-hearted in their freedom of friendship.

His work began immediately after a marriage festival in Cana of Galilee. Somebody has said that no one would have dreamed of inviting John the Baptizer to a wedding, but it was natural that Christ should be bidden to the feast; everyone knew that he would add to the joy of the occasion.

This criticism of John is overstrained; he was probably devoid of a sense of humor, but he was not necessarily a kill-joy. Unquestionably, however, there is real truth in the estimate of Christ's character. Sometimes the ecclesiastics felt that he was altogether too friendly. He mixed too much with all sorts and conditions of people; he received sinners and ate with them too frequently; he failed to rebuke the woman of the city who came to Simon's feast and his host was distressed and perplexed at what seemed to him a lax and easy-going indifference; he permitted one of his own chosen apostles to gather an extraordinarily disreputable company of friends to meet him at dinner. It comes with something of a shock to read that some of his critics actually called him a glutton and a winebibber.

Jesus could also be severe when occasion required. Nothing that John ever said was so biting as the woes the Lord pronounced against the Pharisees. The Baptizer came to his death because of his stern denunciation of Herod's adulterous union; but Jesus also sent a sharp message to the tetrarch, "Go and tell that fox." But his hatred of sin never made his goodness seem warped.

His public life began with the choice of a few intimate friends and most of his public teaching was given while he went with them on pilgrimages through Galilee, the north country from which most of his friends came. He rejoiced in the friendship of the twelve. When questioned about their apparent lack of strict observance of the rules of fasting, he smiled and declared that they could not fast when they were as happy as friends of a newly wed bridegroom.

Nor was his friendship one in which he gave all, and asked, and really needed, nothing. That destroys his humanness. He seems to have greatly needed friends, so thoroughly human was his hunger for their understanding, their affection, their sympathy and support. There is the desire for such understanding, when he asks of Peter, "Who do men say that I am? Who do you say that I am?" There is longing as well as reproach in the words, "Could ye not watch with me one hour?" There trembles on his lips the hesitating fear of one who dreads the solitude of failure, when he asks, "Will you also go away?"

He needed friends—and he had them: Mary and Martha and Lazarus, in whose home affection always gave him a welcome opportunity for relaxation; Peter and James and John, who were a little closer to him than any of the rest of the twelve; most of all, John, who reclined on his breast at supper, the best-beloved disciple, into whose care he commended his mother in the hour of parting. Children were among his good friends. He loved them and they loved him. He watched them at play in the public square with amusement and delight and afterward called attention to their songs. One of them he took on his knees as he talked to his disciples of the need of the childlike spirit in the life of religion. Mothers brought their babies to him, that he might hold them in his arms and bless them.

He had a wonderful capacity for making friends with all sorts of people. Nicodemus took his courage in his hands to go for a quiet talk with him, even though he went after dark. The woman of Samaria involuntarily opened her heart to him. There were even women of Herod's court in the groups which gathered to hear him and afterward joined his company. A wealthy citizen of Jerusalem came forward in the tragic hour of his death to proclaim his friendship and offer a place in which to bury the body of the defeated leader.

There are several stories of the way in which Jesus made friends, but none more full of color than the account of his winning of Zacchæus. Zacchæus was a profiteer; more than that, a grafting governmental profiteer. He was head of the department for the collection of internal revenue in the district of Jericho, and like other tax gatherers had lined his pockets with commissions, not all of them honestly levied. As a Jew who had accepted the office of tax collector under the hated Roman government, he was despised by his people. Yet he was not altogether a bad man; he had a spark of patriotism still burning in his heart, or he would not have been so curious to see, on his way through Jericho, the man who was thought to be the Messiah. Because he was little of stature, Zacchæus climbed up into a tree to look over the heads of the crowd and see Jesus. He was really a ridiculous object—one may suppose that the boys in the crowd tittered, the girls giggled, the adults (who had paid their taxes) sneered at him.

Then Jesus passed by and looked up and seeing

him said, "Hurry now, Zacchæus, and come down; I must be your guest at dinner today." No wonder Zacchæus was a changed man. "Here I am," he thought, "a miserable money grubber, heaping up a fortune without much thought of how I get the money or what I shall do with it. But this man believes in me. Here before the crowd he asks me to be his host. Today, then, I make a new start. Half of my fortune I will give away in charity and every false collection of taxes I will pay back four times over. This man trusts me and makes me his friend and I mean to live up to his expectations."

Another anecdote which tells of a rich young man who came to Jesus adds that "when he saw him, Jesus loved him." It was of this man that the extraordinary demand was made, "Go, sell all that thou hast, and give to the poor." Some have explained the unusual injunction on the assumption that it was an offer of closer friendship, with perhaps appointment to apostleship. If so, the refusal is indeed the record of "a great rejection."

The twelve companions and their Master, and possibly some of the others with them on occasions, went through the fields and along the friendly road, while he talked with them and now and then taught those who gathered about the little company. As he taught, God and goodness became very real.

A number of men met recently in the smoking car of a train in which they were traveling on their way to New York. They talked of the business in hand and of the pleasures in prospect, when one of them said that he feared he would be kept in the city till the end of the week. The others began to congratulate him on the happy prospect; whereupon he broke forth: "Nobody knows how I hate it; how I dislike the pushing and crowding at the station, the mad rush of the subway, the jam in the stores, the crowds in the hotel lobbies, the mobs pouring out of the theaters, the procession of automobiles on the avenue, the careering and adventurous taxicabs—everybody in a hurry to go somewhere and not quite sure why they are hurrying nor where they would arrive. Nobody knows how I want to get away from the sight of men digging into the bowels of the earth to make place for new lines of transportation, or tearing down fine old houses to build apartments, or climbing into the sky to erect buildings big enough to house all the people of my own town. Back home," he sighed, "there is room to breathe and time to think. We have the hills and the water and the trees—and 'only God can make a tree.' I have a chance to feed the intellectual life a little. I can live now and then in the spirit. I can even, once in a while, think about God."

And so those happy companions on the friendly road thought about God, in the peace of the simple life, as their Master told story after story, each with its special lesson, thus gradually making them understand the whole body of his teaching, slowly bringing them to think of God as Friend and Father, even as he himself was Friend and Brother.

As they came to know Jesus better, they were amazed to discover how he could read their hearts. Nothing seemed hidden from him. On the day when the first disciples were introduced to him, they felt that he was reading them through and through as he asked their reason for following him.

The next day Simon was greeted with the words: "I know you; you are Simon, the son of Jonas. I know your father; I know your early environment; I know your present feelings; I know your weakness and impulsiveness. But I also know your future possibilities. I mean to call you Peter, the Rock-Man."

The following day Nathanael was astonished, when Philip brought him to Jesus, to find that he, too, was known. "Look! an Israelite indeed; a frank, free, open-hearted Jew." "Why, how is it that you know me?" Nathanael asked. "Before Philip called you, while you were under the fig tree, I saw you." Just what the words meant to Nathanael we do not know, whether he had spread his praying mat under the shade of the tree and now saw in the new Master's eyes knowledge of what his prayers had been about; whether he realized that Jesus knew all about his scornful reference, later, to the little good that might be expected to come out of Nazareth—what it was we do not know, but he must have felt, in some way, that his soul was in open view to Jesus, for he cried: "Rabbi! Thou art the Son of God; thou art the King of Israel."

So Jesus knew all men. Matthew, the collector of customs near Capernaum, sat in his taxing booth. Was he thinking of the ideas he caught from the caravans whose toll he collected, drinking in their talk of other nations and other religions, wondering whether there could be an all-inclusive religion that would bring men together in worship of the one Father, driven to his new thoughts because as a tax collector he felt the isolation of his own race and was a little ashamed of their narrow provincialism? Was it then, just at the psychological moment, that Jesus called him, and did he follow because he felt that the man who called him knew all?

And how well Jesus understood the others:

Philip, dull and doubting and slow; Thomas, in whom belief and doubt struggled so constantly that there seemed to be special significance in his nickname, "Didymus," or the Twin; Thaddæus, about whom we know next to nothing.

It was the same with many others. He read the secrets of the soul of the woman of Samaria who met him at the well, who, when she discovered that he knew all about her loose life, ran back to the city, crying, "Come, see a man who told me all things I have ever done. He cannot really be the Christ, can he?" When some of the Jews dragged to him the woman taken in adultery, he looked at them with his "eyes of flame" as he asked any one who was without sin to hurl the first stone; and they went away, one by one, feeling that there was nothing in their lives hid from him.

In the first days of the discipleship of his earliest friends, after an indignant clearing out of the temple traffic, recorded in St. John, and the enthusiastic support of the crowd who loved just such aggressive action, we read that "many believed in his name." The disciples, thereupon, evidently expected immediate acceptance and success. It was only the first of many disappointments, but this time they themselves soon saw that he had read aright the weakness and instability of the proffered support. John says: "Jesus did not commit himself to them, because he knew all men, and needed not that any should bear witness as to the man with whom he was dealing, for he knew what was in man—he could read thoughts and feelings as yet unexpressed."

Chapter VII: Strong Son of God

HAT was it in Jesus that so seized upon his followers that they left all and followed him? How did they come to find in him the master of their souls? What caused their belief in him to grow with such amazing bounds that they ended by putting him in the place of God and giving him the honor due only to divinity?

The answer is beyond dispute. To quote one whose own profession of faith does not go the full extent of the creedal confessions: "The immediate effect of the teaching of Jesus was an effect of power, of authority and mastery, the compelling impressiveness of a leader of men. It is the note of strength. His ministry was dynamic, commanding, authoritative. His dominant trait is force. He has the quiet consciousness of mastery, the authority of the leader; for softness and sentimentality, such as characterizes 'the feminine man,' there was no room in his rugged, nomadic, homeless life."

This impression of mastery, we are reminded, confronts us from whatever side we approach the life of Christ. We see it in the ethical aspect

[64]

of strength and in the intellectual aspect of the
same quality of power—"a strength of reasoning,
a sagacity of insight, an alertness of mind, which
gave him authority over the mind not less than
the will." We are thinking now, however, in a
simpler way of the masterful Christ. We are
thinking of his quiet consciousness of power as
that of a man who held sway over the souls of
others by the force of a strong personality, simple, manly, honest, courageous, true.

Perhaps some of us need an introduction to the
real Jesus Christ. For years we have been learning many things of him which are true, indeed,
and never to be forgotten, but which make up
only one element of his many-sided character.
We have been taught of his tenderness, his gentleness, his meekness; we know of his love and
his long-suffering; but we need to be introduced
to the Christ who was master of men and held
all the vital forces of a complete manhood in re-
serve for any emergency. The thing which first
drew men to him was his power, his forcefulness
of personality, his commanding strength.

This is a side of the character of Jesus which
specially needs re-emphasizing in our day. Youth
in revolt will never be won merely by patience,
meekness, gentleness. It does appreciate robust
and masterful strength, especially if touched with

idealism. That sort of leadership may have for it a romantic attraction.

Think, for example, of Calvary as youth would see it. There is the soldier at the foot of the cross who was won to faith as Christ died. He was a centurion of the Roman guard, detailed to oversee the arrangements for the execution——a rough, plain man whose mind did not turn naturally to spiritual things, who had known little and cared less about the ecclesiastical disputes among the Jews which led to the Good Friday morning trial. There he stood, impatient for the end, ready to go back and make his report when it was all over. He had given little thought to what the whole matter was about, and he looked on, at first, just curiously. But whatever else he did not know, at least he knew a man when he saw him; and when he had seen Christ die, there awoke in this rough man of battle the essence of faith. "Truly," he said, "this was the Son of God." Christianity is concentrated for a moment on these two men——Christ on the cross and the Roman captain looking on——and when the one whose trade had to do with death saw in the dying man, not weakness, but strength, no sign of anything save a power that strangely moved and stirred him, Christ won.

One may look into the mind of the penitent thief and see his response to the same compelling power. He was, possibly, a young man who had become a member of one of the insurrectionist or robber bands that infested the country near Jerusalem. As a youth, he had been captivated by the bold spirit of the leader of such a band; eventually he had joined his company—perhaps out of pure love of adventure, perhaps out of boyish worship of its daring leader, perhaps because his imagination had been fired by some tale of a social wrong that had made his hero an outcast. Now he had come to the end of his mistaken career, and he was dying on the cross. Next him hung this fellow prisoner. He knew something of Christ's claims and had heard of his career. He watched the prisoner; and as he watched, slowly he came to see that all his old hero worship had been misplaced. Here was a hero who could inspire his moral respect: courageous, but large-hearted as well as brave; magnanimous, and always bearing himself in a big way. Christ excited in him a love and loyalty that sprang from a sense of his greatness of heart and splendid manliness. Then the thief saw something more, the power that shone through the Lord's weakness, and in a flash recognized his royalty and passed on to quick faith. "Lord, remember me, when thou comest into thy kingdom."

Jesus Christ was so great in every moment of

his life that it is no wonder men gave him ready allegiance. His words were always with power. His life was like his words; his death, like his life.

There are many today who need to be shown Christ in just that way. There was nothing weak or unmanly about him, and there is nothing small or narrow about his religion. He is, indeed, all that we have been taught to picture him in his meekness and lowliness. He was the Lamb of God, who patiently suffered for the sins of men. He was as tender and compassionate as the gentlest woman. No one who has visited a hospital ward will wish to forget that all the care shown there is the fruit of Christian love and a reflection of the mind of the compassionate Christ. Yes, Jesus is all that we have been told in his tender pity. He wept at the grave of Lazarus and was not ashamed of his tears. He stretched out his hand and touched the leper, who had not felt the warmth and pressure of a human hand since his loathsome disease came upon him. He went about through the Galilean countryside, by his gracious influence softening men's ills, healing their sicknesses, soothing and comforting their distress. We think of him—and rightly—as the Good Shepherd, carrying the lambs in his bosom.

Yes, all of that he was—and we must never

forget it. But he had also the strength of the strongest manhood. He was gentle—yes; but the strong man can always be a gentle man. He was meek and lowly—yes, in disciplined and trustful dependence on his Father. He was no mere quiet visionary, no sadly contemplative saint. He was, as Tennyson says, the "Strong Son of God." He was called the "Master" and men called him such because it was true; he was indeed master of their souls.

The strength of the best manhood is not mere brute force, it is quiet confidence of power. And because Christ was this kind of man, his whole ministry was a ministry of power. That was the reason why men, when they looked up into his face, obeyed. He called them from their homes, their boats, their tax booths, and they gave heed to his call and followed. If women were drawn to him with peculiar loyalty'of devotion, it was partly because women as well as men are won by masterful personalities. How marvelously he combined all that is best in woman and all that is best in man! He had patient endurance and he had wonderful forcefulness, the power to suffer and the power to defy. He was the one man who has combined the beauty of womanly tenderness with the strength of sturdiest manhood. In the same hymn in which we sing of him as "Jesus meek and gentle," we call him "Son of God most high."

Take a few instances: He is "led as a lamb to the slaughter"; but "he set his face steadfastly to go to Jerusalem"; a man's man, with a man's most splendid courage, facing an all-too-certain fate and facing it with such resoluteness that as his disciples followed they "were amazed and were afraid." He weeps in love and pity over Jerusalem; but in the temple he is terrible, as with his whip of rushes he drives out those who are defiling its courts with noisy trade. He prays in Gethsemane in an agony of emotion; but when he steps out of the garden, the crowd of soldiers quail before his stern glance. He is all gentleness to the woman who is a sinner; but he stands face to face with the Pharisees and is unsparing in his denunciation—his words bite and burn and they are flung in the very teeth of the men who have power to drive him to death. Little children love to be near him and are unafraid in his presence; but his message to Herod begins, "Go and tell that fox." Even his opponents recognize his fearlessness: "Master, we know that you are true and care for no man: neither do you have regard for the persons of men."

This picture of Christ the man is very natural and human. If he was that sort of man, then of course he was not demonstrative and gushing—God save us from thinking that mere effusiveness is ever going to attract men to religion—he had dignity as well as strength. Nor, on the other hand, was he narrow and censorious; no true man is. He was not sad and sombre, but natural and spontaneous. He was glad and free, an out-of-doors man who loved people, was genial and companionable, unaffected, fond of the society of his day, meeting people of all sorts in the hearty comradeship of common life, likable and lovable, genuine, generous, largehearted, straightforward, and strong.

We have all of us known men who have an unconfessed but very apparent dislike for religion just because they cannot admire the kind of goodness they think Christianity asks them to admire. They do not see that Christ, with his eager delight in life, with his frank and alert interest in the common affairs of common people, with his buoyancy of spirit, has shown us that we can be good without ceasing to be natural; especially, that we can be good without being miserable; and above all (though we shall come to that later) that our God is the kind of God who is just like Christ.

The Christian character is two-sided. It has softness and it has strength; self-renunciation and self-expression. It is the two-sided character of the Jesus who was meek and lowly, but was also the "Strong Son of God." Its humility is the humility of him who could bend to the task of a slave and gird himself and wash his disciples' feet, just because he was so great, just because he knew that he came forth from God and went to God. The Christian character, in its meekness and gentleness, is the upgrowth of moral greatness; its power is the fruit of its peace. It is rooted and grounded in self-sacrificing love.

And yet—because this foundation robs what rises from it of all self-interest and self-seeking— the Christian character that issues out of this self-surrender, if it is to grow to perfection, must be daring and impetuous, vehement and intense.

It is just here that we have failed. We have softened and weakened our Christianity and left out the heroic, instead of trying to disentangle the heroic from all that is brutal and boastful. We have supposed the Christian life to mean patient submission, with passions subdued and vehemence moderated, instead of learning that vehemence and strength and passion and earnestness must still be there, only liberated and detached from self-assertion and self-seeking. We have forgotten that the spirit of Christ is always a challenge to the heroic. What shames us, what humiliates our Lord, what makes anti-Christian cults grow apace, is that we have allowed our

Christianity to become so shrunken and withered, so mean and unheroic, so comfortable and commonplace, so little like the splendid self-sacrifice of our leader. If we are indeed his followers, we must have hearts of tremendous purpose, a very passion for righteousness, an intense and burning zeal, an unflinchingly persistent determination to live true to the highest and best, a willingness to do and to dare, if need be, to suffer and endure and die.

Chapter VIII: Teaching by the Roadside

T IS impossible, in the short compass of this book, to give a detailed account of the life of Jesus Christ, much less an adequate study of his teaching. All that we are trying to do is to create an atmosphere in which his life and teaching may be studied, if one is eager to know more.

Few people now read "the old, old story" as it was read by our fathers. They were accustomed to read religious books to the exclusion of many others; they talked about religion frequently, studied their Bibles daily, remembered texts and sermons as something of vital worth, and were more or less compelled to yield to a pervading religious ideality. This persistent living, as it used to be said, under "the droppings of the gospel," gave character to their thought, molded their daily attitudes and activities, and prepared them for further realizations of the divine.

It may be questioned whether, on the whole, there is not greater honesty and more downright sincerity in the expression of religious thought today; yet it cannot be disputed that something is lacking. There was an "atmosphere" of religion in those days which we miss now. One feels, in telling the story of Jesus Christ, that nothing can be taken for granted; it is not safe to assume familiarity with any details of the narrative. On the other hand, perhaps the fuller knowledge of the story in other days was also a hindrance. It was an old, old story, heard so often that it did not often hush the heart into reverence. It could be heard without one's feeling its wonder.

If it were only possible to read the narrative with the freshness of interest given to a new story, the beauty and charm of it could not fail to move the reader. There would still be difficulties, of course, but they would not loom so large; the story has all the *naïveté* of the record of eyewitnesses, telling what they saw, sometimes giving explanations that possibly would not be natural for us, but writing as men who lived in the wonder of a soul-stirring experience. In his dealings with his disciples, Jesus was making to them the great suggestion: "You need God." There is a hunger of the human heart for God. One by one, the disciples felt the longing to know him better. One by one, they capitulated to Christ, they fell under His spell, they "gave in" to God and surrendered themselves to Him. They made Christ their master and definitely declared for him against the world. The gospels tell of their experience and tell of it in such a way as

[75]

to bear plainly the evidence of their honesty and of the general reliability of their witness.

In the informal teaching which he gave by the roadside, Jesus spoke of God in the simple language of simple, everyday people, usually in short stories with homely illustrations out of their common life. One can quite understand how the truths he gave would move the hearts of men to whom his language and thought were new, instead of being so familiar as to seem commonplace. The men who reported his talks may occasionally fail in a meticulous accuracy, but in general they are reliable interpreters, as they are honest witnesses.

The power of Christ's parables lies in the harmony felt by most men between the natural world and the spiritual; they trace natural laws in the spiritual realm, on the assumption that the world of nature and the world of grace come from the same hand. Things on earth are copies of the things of heaven, and we learn more of spiritual laws as we examine lovingly the observed laws of the natural world. This will be seen more especially in the parables of the kingdom. In other parables a similar harmony is suggested between human life and thought and God's ways and work.

Certain fundamental ideas recur again and again in Christ's teaching. The first is unfaltering faith in the Fatherhood of God. If God is our Father, we can trust ourselves to His care, without anxious thought of the morrow. The parable of the lost sheep shows His care for each individual soul and His anxious labor to recover every one who has strayed from Him. The parable of the lost piece of silver shows that His children are lost, often, through no fault of their own; and that then, too, He seeks with the same unfailing diligence to restore them. The most touching of all the stories is that of the prodigal son, a wayward, impatient, "heady" young man, who tired of the humdrum life of the home, took his inheritance, and left to go "on his own" in the venturesome life of the larger world. He made a tragic failure of the experiment and returned, humble and penitent, willing to begin again on the lowest round of life's ladder, and finding his father ready to receive him with open arms and to help him back to self-respect. The contrast between the father's forgiveness and the older brother's severity of judgment is a vivid picture of an experience common to every age; for "safe" men are usually hard in their judgments, and good men are often hardest of all, especially if their goodness be, as it is likely to be with safe men, the plodding fidelity of a heart naturally but uninspiringly responsive to duty and yet so satisfied with its own achievement as to be unconscious that this hard and unimaginative adherence to duty may be less acceptable than the blundering service of one who loves much.

The fatherhood of God implies the brotherhood of men in God's family. Some of the Lord's parables teach human brotherhood in stories that will never grow old. Who can fail to see the lesson in the story of the beggar Lazarus and the rich man who gave no thought to the poor at his door? Who can miss the meaning of the tale of the Samaritan merchant and the man who fell among thieves, receiving help, not from the "good" people who saw his distress, churchmen both of them, but from the despised outsider?

Then there are stories to show what the service of God should mean. The man of many talents may never have learned the motto, *noblesse oblige*. The man with one talent may forget that service is required even of the humblest, because God takes account of circumstances, environment, poverty of opportunity. And in contrasting the highly placed and the poorly equipped, we need to remember the "two-talent men," ordinary, common folk who have duties and obligations quite as important for them as are those of the more privileged genius with many talents.

The world seems to think that power and influence may excuse indifference to the weak, and riches be expected to make a man hard, and that because a man has talent he will probably be careless of innocence and delightfully nonmoral. Men so often use their advantages to build about themselves a wall of privilege. What Christ says is the very opposite: The more power a man has, the more sympathetic he should be; the richer he is, the more abounding should be his generosity; because he has culture, he must be the more careful not to lose touch with common folk; because he is a genius, he ought to be better than other men. The real privilege of power is not that it may excuse us from irksome duties and lift us above human needs and sympathies, but that it makes it possible for us to enter more fully into life, know more of the world, have a wider experience, and so share more burdens, do more work, accept larger responsibilities and be finer men and women.

If that were not plainly enough taught in the parables of Jesus, it was made clear beyond any possible misunderstanding in the "parable in action" which is recorded among the events of the Last Supper, when "Jesus, knowing that the Father had given all things into his hands, and that he was come from God, and went to God; he rose from supper, and laid aside his garments, and took a towel, and girded himself, and poured water into a basin, and began to wash his disciples' feet." Just because he was so great, no task could possibly lower or debase him. Because he came from God, he could minister to men. Because he was a son, he could, without any loss of dignity, do a servant's work.

One thing, Christ said, is needful—to put first things first and place the service of God above every other obligation. That is the meaning of his words to the rich young man, who might have been an apostle, but could not become one unless he were willing to part with his wealth and take his place with the others in a common brotherhood where the presence of a specially favored member would have destroyed real fellowship.

One thing is needful; and the rich fool discovered this when he had spent his life in the accumulation of property and then suddenly learned that he must appear at once to render his account to God, from whom his life came.

One thing is needful; and if privileges are not used in God's service they may be taken away—so we are taught in the parable of the pounds, in the story of the barren fig tree, in the fate of the unprofitable servants.

One thing is needful, faithful service, which receives its blessing even when rendered during the very close of opportunity, as with the laborers in the vineyard; even when offered at last, after much grudging and hot-headed protest, by one who (like the boy in the parable of the two sons) fights against duty but finally answers the call of conscience. One wonders how many young people today are like this boy, defiant and rebellious, yet sound at heart!

Among the worst sins are the sins of indifference. The story of the feast which the invited guests declined to attend, excusing their absence as busy business men today excuse their neglect to cultivate the things of the spirit, plainly declares that. So does the story of the marriage of the king's son, with its added warning that spiritual privileges may not only be neglected, but may be accepted with an irreverent nonchalance quite as offensive.

Men must live in constant recognition of their accountability to God. Their Master may come most unexpectedly, as when the bridegroom's sudden arrival found the bridesmaids unprepared for the wedding procession. When He comes, His judgment on contemptuous indifference and opposition will be severe—for God is just, as well as merciful, as the wicked husbandmen learned to their cost. If we desire mercy from Him, we must show the spirit of mercy to others—this is the lesson of the story of the two debtors, as it is the prayer of the great model of devotion:

"Forgive us our trespasses, as we forgive those who trespass against us."

We are earth-bound, all of us, and the world is very alluring; but even its temptations and entice-ments may be turned into opportunities, for we may "make to ourselves friends of the mammon of unrighteousness." The parable of the unjust steward is full of difficulties. Is it really intended to teach business men that there is a way of doing business, while yet following Christ?

Two of the longer stories Jesus told have fired the imagination of all time: the parable of the prodigal son and the elder brother, and the para-ble of the Pharisee and the publican. These have always been regarded as peculiarly typical of Christ's thought, giving full expression to his ideas of religion and life.

It may be doubted whether most of those who admire the stories for their beauty have thought very deeply of some of their implications. One can quite see how the story of the forgiven prodi-gal would appeal to an age that is only too glad to think of God as a loose, lax, kindly, benevolent Deity, who regards sin as an unfortunate mistake easily overlooked. As a matter of fact, the point of the story would seem to be quite different. Studied closely, it does more than tell of the heav-enly Father's patience; it describes two types of character: the class of people to whom religion seems narrow and belittling as compared with the broader ways of the world, who are in no way conscious of the need of divine grace, who see no reason for self-discipline, but think it rather fine and free and splendid to follow any urge and thus avoid morbid self-consciousness; second, the class of people who live a sheltered life and desire nothing different, whose creed is the latter part of the *Gloria Patri* ("As it was in the beginning, is now, and ever shall be, world without end"), whose special danger is that of narrowness, who set up tests and standards based only on their own experience, whose temptations are not towards impatience and revolt, but towards a self-engrossed piety.

One might discover in the parable a special application in present-day life. Today youth is in revolt, but age is not altogether lovely! And youth can learn only by experience. The intense attraction of an undisciplined life may in the end teach the worth of some things that once were despised. God is patient because God understands. He will understand even if, in after days, there are memories of a past that still haunt us. Youth is impatient and age is often narrow and self-satisfied, cramped, unsympathetic, unresponsive. Which—the impatient youth or the contented man of settled habits—is more likely to "come to himself" and go in penitence to the Father?

The parable of the Pharisee and the publican presents special difficulties, clear as its meaning seems to be on first thought. There is nothing of the kindly and benevolent God in the language Christ uses of the Pharisees! His attitude toward them, as a class, presents a remarkable contrast to the way in which he treated others. In general, he always saw latent possibilities of good where they were least expected; he seemed, instinctively, to draw the best out of people. But for the pharisaical spirit his language was that of stern denunciation, even of scornful contempt.

The strange thing about it is not merely that he who speaks in this way is the same teacher who had the greatest patience with the most degraded type of sinners and never uttered a word that would lead them to despise themselves or to despair of themselves. No, there is something more unaccountable: he speaks with this extreme of severity of those who were the "good people" of their day, who were seen constantly at prayer, were never-failing in the observance of religious rites, were leaders in the life of their church, and were probably pointed out as deserving of all praise and respect.

What, then, was wrong with them? Why

should they have been the one class for which even Christ's patience could not be enlarged? Why were his dealings with them at variance with his attitude toward others? The answer is that in the Pharisee there was nothing to which Christ could appeal. Just so long as the voice of conscience has not been wholly silenced, so long as there is an occasional sting of self-condemnation, so long as there are some restless longings, love may draw out the better self; but all these were absent with the Pharisee and therefore the only possible thing was to sting him with contempt, in the hope that at last he might be stung into self-contempt.

The supreme sin of the Pharisees, as a class, lay in the fact that they had nothing to regret, nothing to desire, no aims they had not reached. They were so sure of their own goodness and so convinced of the worth of their regulatory system, that their one passion was to enforce the law for others. They approved of the wrath of God against sin, but it was the sin of other people, not their own. They were hardened in self-righteousness. Their consciences could but "echo the vain approval of self-deceit." The Pharisee of the parable felt that he had nothing to repent of; he accused himself of no fault, great or small; he had left nothing undone which he ought to have done. He was perfectly satisfied with himself. How could such a man ever be made to feel the need of redeeming grace?

All of this we see in the parable, in one short, sharp sentence which tells the whole story in a line. It gives a plain answer to the question as to why Christ found this type of mind hopelessly unresponsive to the means and methods by which he sought to win others.

He doubtless feels exactly the same about the Pharisees of today; only it is well to remember that it ill behooves us to lay claim to any measure of his insight into human hearts; and therefore few of us care or dare to point out individuals who need to be stung into real faith, rather than won. Even Christ pointed his denunciations at a class, not at individuals. For the most part, men are usually better than the mistaken organizations with which they are identified.

Chapter IX: The Church and the Kingdom

HE Jews never lost hope of a great destiny for their nation. Unlike other peoples who looked back to a golden age in the past, their hope lay in the future. The Jew was an inveterate optimist. At times he and his faith in God were ground to powder by the cruel course of history. A small nation, in the midst of mighty empires, the Hebrew people felt to the quick all the sharp actualities of life. They saw their nation fail of its opportunities and fall; they saw it rise and for a while go stumbling onward; they saw it fall again, and in the time of Christ become a subject nation, a little province of a great empire—yet their hope never died, and even in the darkest days a remnant of the people kept alive their sensitive faith.

When Jesus was proclaimed as the Messiah, hope sprang into new life for many eager patriots and earnest seekers after righteousness. After the death of John, "Jesus came into Galilee preaching the good news of God: The time is fulfilled, and the kingdom of God is at hand." Again and again, some patriotic radical sought to crown him as king; again and again, he frustrated their plans. Yet he kept on "preaching the kingdom." Many of his parables set forth his interpretation of the hope of Israel.

Controversy has always been keen, and often bitterly contentious, as to the meaning of the Jewish hope and the use which Jesus made of the national expectation. If we can forget controversy and read afresh his teaching, we shall find it much more simple than academic interpreters have supposed.

All the hopes and expectations of the Jews found expression in the one word, the "Kingdom." What, then, had their own prophets taught them of this pregnant word, before Jesus came? First came their expectation of a great future for the nation. They looked for a second David who would restore the old glory. Gradually this national hope was united, under the teaching of the prophets, with the idea of the eventual supremacy of God. The Kingdom would be His sovereignty in the world, with all nations subject to His rule of righteousness. This meant that the new David would rule over a new people, his kingdom a righteous kingdom.

Then, as generations passed and empires rose and fell, with God's rule still unacknowledged, Jewish thought turned to the vision of Daniel and looked for a national regeneration in which the kingdoms of the world would be broken to pieces and "the saints of the Most High" have dominion in an everlasting kingdom that would "stand forever." Slowly the facts of history led many to see that no conception of a new Israel which rested on world sovereignty held promise of fulfilment, and so the day of restoration was postponed to the end of time. Only in the culmination of all things, when God came to judge the world, would the hope of Israel be fulfilled.

When Jesus began to teach, there were, in general, two ideas current: one, the somewhat crude idea of deliverance from alien rule and the establishment of Jewish independence under a righteous king; the other, the expectation that the great day of judgment was at hand and that God would come as judge in the person of a supernatural being, representing Him and anointed with His Spirit. No wonder all men marveled of Jesus, whether he were the Christ! Was he the king who would make them masters of the world? Or was one great period of the world's history drawing to a close, and was Jesus the Anointed One who would sweep away evil and bring in a new order? And, if the latter, would he establish a kingdom on earth in which the redeemed would enjoy all possible happiness? Would this reign of righteousness endure for a mystical millennial period, and would there come at its end a new day, with new heavens and a new earth, an eternal day of future life with God forever?

The people in general, especially the radical people of Galilee, some of whom were eager for a revolution, looked for a temporal ruler. From time to time there had been threatened revolts under false Messiahs, all of them ending in failure. The more religious had hope of a righteous kingdom, in which, perhaps, a great Messiah-King would reign as God's vicegerent. They hardly knew how his sway would reach to all nations, but they hoped, and some of them prayed. Probably a chosen few, such as the aged Simeon, who had held Jesus in his arms when the child was presented in the temple, had vague longings for a time when men would own individual allegiance to God and give their hearts to Him in faithful service. They began to see that the day of the Lord must be a day of personal consecration. They "waited for the consolation of Israel" and "spoke to all those who looked for redemption in Jerusalem."

It is the last thought that gives the clue to the teaching of Jesus. This appealed to the imagination even of those who did not quite understand it. He was always interesting, and because his teaching was so simple and picturesque, in story form, with many references to incidents of actual life, it always attracted plain people.

Interesting, let it be repeated, even for those who did not understand; for he was a true teacher, aiming to drive home his ideas to a few kindred souls—those who could not be content without his own full explanation of the story—but willing to let the ideas rest as seed thoughts in minds where they would germinate more slowly. Hearing, they would hear, but not yet understand.

So we have his parables of the kingdom. Look! A sower sowing his seed. See where it falls. Some drops on the trodden path, some on shallow earth which barely covers the rock, some amid the thorns and briers along the edge of the field, some in the good soil. What is the Kingdom? It is the implanted word of God, the message of God as spoken, but still awaiting its full reception. When will the Kingdom come? When men hear and heed the message. Some men have trivial minds, and the word will make no impression on them; some are shallow, with no deep convictions; some so engrossed with the work and pleasures of life that the better nature is stifled. There is nothing spectacular about the coming of the Kingdom. It all depends on the growth of the word in men's hearts. It must fall on good ground if it is to bring forth fruit to perfection. The Kingdom is the reign of God in men's hearts, as they hear His word and follow it. It is like growing seed.

When will the Kingdom come? Very slowly, but come it will, as the tree grows from the tiny seed. Progress will seem small. The seed grows secretly. But the progress is sure. There will be a little community of the faithful, but it will become a great company and in it men will find rest for their souls. It is like the seed from which rises a great tree, in whose branches the birds have their homes.

Will it change the world? Surely, even as the leaven makes the dough a living lump.

What must we do to bring in the Kingdom? Give up everything, that you may find it. It is like treasure hid in a field. If one knows it is there, he will buy the field at heavy cost. It is like a pearl of great price. When the merchant discovers it, he will sell all to secure it.

All these parables show the Kingdom as a principle of life, a law of conduct—the acceptance of God's will, the reign of God in the heart. But because it is this, it will have its outward manifestation—a new spirit working in the world, with a community of the faithful giving it definite and visible form. There one begins to see

the idea of the church, as the nucleus of the Kingdom. The church is God's tree of life, a homing
place for souls.

Yes; well, then, may we look soon for a time
when all will be faithful? No; the Kingdom is
like a field with tares among the wheat. And
you cannot separate the tares from the good
grain, lest you root up the wheat with the weeds.
The Kingdom will have its bad citizens, as the
net gathers fish, some good and some of no value.
There one finds the church, again, with all its
strength and all its weakness, its faithful members and its faithless.

When will disloyalty cease and all men do
righteously? Only in the day of the consumma-
tion of all things, just as the tares are not separated from the wheat until the time of harvest;
and as the good and bad fish are placed in different heaps when the net is drawn in and the catch
counted.

Three conceptions of the church, one sees, and
all consistent: The Kingdom, the Word of God
in the heart of man; the Kingdom, the company
of the faithful who have received the word,
though some, even of these, prove unworthy; the
Kingdom, the church triumphant, with the will
of God supreme and the righteous shining forth
as the sun—the Kingdom of God within you; the

Kingdom visible in a society; the Kingdom come in full power at the great day.

In the parable of the wheat and the tares, as well as in that of the dragnet, full of fishes good and bad, we find the thought of the Kingdom as a divine society, faulty because its membership is made up of faulty humanity. Do we find the church idea, that is, the idea of Christianity as a corporate, not a purely individual life, in the further teaching of Jesus as we follow him in his general purpose?

Of course he was all that the devoutest imagination can picture him in the simple beauty of his life of service. Of course he did ask, first of all, for personal love and loyalty. Of course the Kingdom begins with the spoken word of God. But while he made men his followers, one by one, apparently he never meant his followers to be left loose and unattached. It seems no less than natural that individual fellowship should be kept strong and steady through corporate union. Individual attachment, of course; but, after that, corporate union for its safeguarding; rather, corporate union in order that the band of individual disciples may become the nucleus of a kingdom and, by moving out into the community, may not merely hold the believer but save the world.

Do we find that in our further study of the

great life? Surely we must seek it there, if we are to have firm belief in the church, a belief that carries atmosphere, courage, conviction. Modern discipleship is hesitating and uncertain just because it lacks this larger vision. We shall always leave the church out of our calculations, if we think of it as the afterthought of men rather than as the forethought of Christ. The church will never be anything but an idea, impotent and unsaving, unless we are sure that Christ himself meant to found a visible society where his life was to be lived in corporate fellowship.

That the organization of such a society was in the mind of the Master seems plain, as we read the rest of the story. This idea of the church as a visible society, which we see in the teaching about the Kingdom, would seem, therefore, to be of the essence of Christian faith. We may almost declare, indeed, that this seems to have been the real purpose of Christ's life: not to do the little good that could be done in those few brief years, in one small corner of the world; but to train a band of men who would understand who and what he was and how his life was to be imparted to others, and would organize a society through which his life would be made known, his death pleaded, and his teaching perpetuated.

And there you do indeed find the purpose—

something revealed at first only to the inner circle of friends; revealed to them gradually, but unmistakably.

Go forward a little to the time when the years of his ministry are drawing to a close. More and more he withdraws from the crowds. A sifting process has been in operation. The seed thoughts of his teaching have found sure lodgment in a few hearts. He begins to train the loyal few with even greater painstaking care. We shall see how he bends all his energies to make them understand the secret of his life. One night he spends in absorbed devotion, and then he asks a momentous question of Peter: "Who do you say that I am?" He waits anxiously for the answer. "The Christ, the Son of the Living God." That is what he has been waiting for, and quickly he declares: "Yes, I have made no mistake about you, Peter; you are indeed a Man of Rock, and on the rock of faith like yours I mean to build my church."

It seems "all of a piece" with what he declared in those early parables. The seed sown, finding lodgment, growing surely. God's will now the law of life. His own office recognized. His own teaching received. His own life understood. His time come to take steps that nothing shall be lost or forgotten. The time ripe to tell of what the future bears in store for him and for them. The day of building near at hand.

That is the conception of Christ's eternal purpose which we need to lay hold upon in these days, when the idea has gone abroad that church membership is a matter of indifference, and church loyalties a matter of choice, and that even if we become members we may make our own church, if we will; the idea that the church is "a mere amorphous aggregation of individual souls, a society through which a set of views may be promulgated—and a more or less incoherent and unstable set of views at that."

Real belief in the church means more than that. To the true churchman, as to the Apostle Paul, the church is the body of Christ, and Christianity is necessarily a life lived in corporate fellowship, its members having direct relation to the living head of the church and through him fellowship with each other.

That idea of the church, also, we find in the later teaching and purpose of Christ himself. Toward the end of his life, he spoke about it more plainly, so we are told in the fourth gospel. Again he taught by parable. This time he told his friends that he was the vine, and they the branches. As the sap flows through the vine out into the branches, quickening and freshening the

[97]

youngest shoots, so his life would flow into their hearts. All this we shall learn more about later; but it must be told now, briefly, if we are to see the church in the teaching and plan of Christ himself.

The church idea is not something which arose out of the accommodation of Christianity to the empire in which the Christian faith spread. It is not found only in the system of Paul, supposed to be the first great churchman. It is discovered to lie in the mind of Christ in his earliest teaching about the kingdom; it is seen to be a prime object of his ministry; its charter is read in the quick response of the Lord to the ardent faith of the spokesman of the apostles: "You are indeed the Rock-Man, and upon the rock of faith like this I will build my church, and all the powers of evil shall never gain the victory over it."

Chapter X: The Social Gospel

O SINCERELY religious people in a not very distant past, "the Kingdom of Heaven" meant assurance of personal salvation and a life of happiness in God's presence hereafter. To others, it has meant a man-to-man and group-to-group movement, creating new influences for good in its progress and strengthening the forces of righteousness. In some such way, many have understood the Lord's Prayer. "Thy will be done" means submission to suffering or loss as God's purpose in particular cases. "Thy kingdom come" expresses longing for the time when sorrow and sighing shall be done away. Or, perhaps, it is a prayer that more people may be faithful in service, and the kingdom come in power.

In the teaching of Christ there is something far greater than this. The Kingdom is the word of God sown in the heart; it is the slow progress of God's law until His will be done on earth as it is done in heaven. Then, over and above that, the "Kingdom of Heaven" seems to mean *organized* righteousness. For this reason, an age which more than previous ages shows a keen

[99]

sense of the injustice and inequalities of the prevailing order of things, has found sympathetic understanding in the teachings of Jesus and in consequence has looked for more of social leadership from the church which claims to speak for him—has looked and has often been disappointed not to find what it seeks.

Can we then see clearly in the words of Christ a social gospel for today? What did he say in which we may discover special meaning for this age, with its complicated social problems and its social sins? Would all his sympathies be with Labor? Would he be a Socialist? An Internationalist? A Pacifist? A Communist? Would he be sympathetic to the Industrial Revolution? Or to the Social Revolution? Would he be anxious for a radical change in family and government? Would he be a Conscientious Objector, should a new war begin tomorrow?

Or, again, is it absurd even to ask such questions? After all, was not his day so different from ours that we actually look to him in vain for any practical guidance in circumstances and relationships which for him were nonexistent?

As a matter of fact, to go still further, does it appear that because he lived so simple a life in so simple an age, his teaching seems a bit dreamy and visionary, the kindly, gentle, other-worldliness of a quiet mystic who knew very little about the hard facts of life, till at last they "smashed" him and put to rout his philosophy of life?

Before we try to answer such questions, it may be well to remember that Jesus did not spend all his days on the friendly road in quiet converse. He spent much of the three years of his public life in city surroundings. Nazareth, where his boyhood days were passed, was a bustling town in Galilee, of 15,000 or perhaps 20,000 population, not far from the principal trade routes. Galilee itself was traversed by two great roads running east and west, over which passed many caravans with the commerce of the East; over which also came, from the west, Roman officials, government embassies and military detachments. Capernaum, where Jesus made his residence almost from the first days of his work, was a busy commercial town, the center of a fish-exporting trade of no mean proportions. It was a military post, of course, with its barracks; fortunately, with a commanding officer who was friendly, possibly "a proselyte of the gate"—for it is recorded that he loved the Jewish people and had built them a synagogue. Not far away was Tiberias, a gay court town where Herod had his palace and his courtesans, his fast society, his fashionable friends, and a civil and military establishment exhibiting all the sins of officialdom in the easy-going East.

Galilee itself was the home of "progressives." The Galilean people were never tamed into quiet submission, as were many of the southern folk. They were like the proud Highlanders of Scotland—indeed, they had a rough dialect with as strong a "burr" in it, by comparison with the speech of Judea, as ever marked the Scotsman's tongue when heard in conversation with Englishmen of smoother speech. Peter's speech betrayed him as a Galilean when he began to swear in the palace the night his Master was taken. In Galilee, the radicals, the patriots, the rebels, the ever-hopeful revolutionists ran riot from time to time. Among the twelve apostles was Simon the Zealot. Galilee had all the freedom and fervency of our exuberant, youthful West, by comparison with the cautious, conservative East.

If there was any "social question," then, in that day, Jesus Christ must have been more than ordinarily conscious of it. And of course there were, in fact, social problems, with all the cruel contrasts of wealth and poverty, as sharply insistent as those of today. Different in type, to be sure; for there was nothing in Galilee (though Rome could tell a different story; and, perhaps, Jerusalem) like the congested life of our great cities;

and the hideous ugliness and sordid surroundings of modern industry were undreamed of.

As indicating that Jesus was alive to what we call social problems, it should be remembered that his forerunner, John the Baptist, put the burden of his teaching just there. The tax gatherers who asked what they must do were told, "Exact no more than is appointed"; or, as we should say, "Cut out all graft." The soldiers were told to avoid violence—perhaps in brutally taking what their wages were not large enough to provide. In general, men were urged to share their prosperity with others. "He that has two coats, let him give to him that has none, and he that has food, let him do likewise." John's preaching was in large measure the preaching of a new kingdom of righteousness.

Jesus took up the teaching in the same spirit, if not always after the same stern and often denunciatory method. Yet almost the first act of his public life was the sharp attack upon the official grafters of the temple, who had let out spaces within the sacred enclosure for their own profit. So unceasing was his sense of indignation at this temple traffic, that he apparently renewed the attack a second time, towards the close of his life, when he drove out the traffickers from the temple courts and overthrew their booths, while they fled terrified before his blazing anger.

He knew, too, the needs of the poor—he had lived with them. We see this, not so much in his words as in what often lies back of his words. Why should he have commended so generously the poor widow who brought unobtrusively to the temple her offering of two "mites," had he not known all the self-sacrifice it represented? Why should he have risked his life—and in the end lost it—by his denunciation of the Pharisees who "devoured widows' houses," had he not felt keenly the oppression of the poor? Had he not seen the "army of unemployed" in some market place? Surely; else we had never heard of the parable of the laborers in the vineyard. He must have known about many a Lazarus, or he could not have pictured so vividly this particular beggar, who dragged himself to the rich man's gate, to receive compassion only from the dogs who licked his sores.

Jesus was not himself a child of poverty. He came of honest, God-fearing, self-respecting, well-descended people of the artisan class. He understood their problems, therefore, as well as the problems of the very poor.

For this reason, also, he never appears as a "class" prophet, conscious only of the trials of the under man and unaware of the difficulties of

the better placed. He knew the rich, as well as
the poor, or the honest middle class. When he
turned to his disciples after the rich young man's
"great refusal," he sighed and said: "How hard
it is for a rich man to enter the kingdom." Indeed, it was like squeezing through the opening
of the "Needle's Eye." He understood, in other
words, that the life of luxury makes for moral
softness; it is tremendously difficult for the man
who lives at ease to be less than well contented
with life as it is. Christ knew well that with
wealth there is likely to come what Robert Louis
Stevenson called "fatty degeneration of the moral
nature."

No wonder, then, that he preached about the
Kingdom of Heaven as a corporate society as
well as a seed of new life; not only as a rule of
righteousness, but as "organized righteousness."

And yet we look to him in vain for any conception of the Kingdom which runs parallel with
some of today's legislation. He seemed to care
little for law as law. One finds nothing in his
teaching to indicate that he would be sympathetic
to the idea that the paramount duty of his church
is the formulating of programs, the engineering
of particular schemes of reform, the utilization
of Christian organization as a political force, or
the employment of his ministers as lobbyists and

propagandist agents in legislative halls. Church and state are different realms, in both of which officers act as "ministers of God" and we must "render unto Caesar the things which are Caesar's and unto God the things which are God's."

Instead of adjudicating in social matters, he showed a singular dislike for interference in particular cases. When one man with a grievance came to him desiring his help in compelling a division of family property, Jesus' first words were an expression of searching insight into the man's soul. It was not so much a matter of zeal for justice that brought him in such a hurry; it was covetous anxiety to get all he could. "Man, who made me a judge or a divider over you? Take heed and beware of covetousness."

Nor was Jesus, in the strict sense of the word, a social reformer. Instead of preaching social revolution, he urged upon all deep searching of the heart, to discover the near-at-hand sin. He did, indeed, speak in scathing denunciation of the sins of the wealthier classes, but he did not go to the opposite extreme of flattering the masses; quite the contrary. Social partisanship in the church or among the clergy today does not represent Christ, and in the end will not win the workers. The minister is in the best possible position to be a mediator between the rich and the poor. Not being overrich himself, and yet rarely falling below a "decent poverty," he has an unusual opportunity to break down class prejudices and create a general social consciousness.

Nor did Christ appear interested in the social question from the standpoint of legislation. We have already seen that in his teaching he always sets forth principles, leaving to us their application, because that is the only way by which we can grow into robust moral strength. So here: he is content to arouse a new social conscience, because he sees that this of itself will solve all problems. Indeed, the strength of his influence lies, in large measure, in this very fact, that he declined to advocate specific reforms; he did something better, he set forth principles which made reform inevitable. Had he been a legislator dealing specifically with local conditions of his own day, his teaching would have been of little value when that day had passed. His method was different; it was to create the sense of individual responsibility.

And today the supreme social duty of the church and of churches is the same: the kindling of brotherly understanding and confidence and the spreading of it as by contagion. Men may conscientiously differ as to methods of social reform, though they are equally concerned about the evils which they seek to eradicate. Remembrance of this would save us many sorrows in our

Christian crusading in America today! There is a clear distinction between moral teaching and the particular social, industrial, economic, or legislative methods by which the moral teaching may be applied to particular problems.

Christ's method has one obvious advantage. The real cause of social disorder, economic evil, industrial injustice, intemperance, poverty, crime —the real cause is found in the passions and ambitions of individual men. We shall never find a system which can guarantee social betterment. No law can be framed which unscrupulous men cannot evade; no social organization can be devised which they cannot in some way utilize to their own ends.

Christ, therefore, worked from within to change individuals. He showed that "the greatest contribution to the social movement is the contribution of a regenerated personality." "What we need is not so much a change of method as a change of heart." Therefore, out of all the disagreements and uncertainties today as to the duty of Christ's church, this fundamental statement may be accepted: Wherever and whenever a moral question arises, it is the function of the church as a corporate society, the kingdom of organized righteousness, to establish the principles upon which the question shall be settled; but it must be left to individuals, acting singly in their capacity as citizens, or united in organizations, to see that right principles are duly expressed in specific reforms.

Perhaps, if he were speaking again today, Jesus would remind us—does he not, in fact, remind us?—that just as the problem of marriage is a matter of right attitude, so it is with social reform. In his teaching about marriage he came closer, apparently, to specific legislative interpretation than in any other moral decision, perhaps because it is of the essence of marriage that there should be reasonable certainty of its permanence; otherwise, at the first serious difference, a break-up would be inevitable. The fact that the life of the family is a life of moral training, a matter of "give and take," a problem in readjustments, an education in unselfishness—all this must be understood. And this may best be practiced, when the injunction is clear that we *must* try, as a family, to preserve family happiness at any cost. We must not be allowed to surrender to the first difficulty, with the thought in the back of our heads that there is always the opportunity of another chance.

The problems of social life and the industrial order can be solved only when the same spirit is carried into the larger relationship. "All ye are brethren" must be the motto of every effort.

The world is a larger family—an immense organization for mutual help—and you must do your part in keeping the family together. This is what Jesus taught; and it was because, in the first centuries, the church of Christ appeared as a brotherly society making the welfare of its members its first and controlling principle, that it made such tremendous strides in the Roman world.

It can make great progress now; but progress will come only as we go "back to Jesus" and seek to learn what his will really is, for his church, for men, for the world. Nowhere will the study be more fascinating and fruitful than in the effort to learn more about the Kingdom, especially in the larger problems of national and of social life. Must a nation be "as good as a good man"? How can a national enemy be forgiven after the same rule as that which commands the curbing of personal resentment? Can the same law hold, when the rights and safety of others must be considered, as well as our own freedom from injury? How can different loyalties be harmonized?

Answers are bound to be different, but truth will prevail when the real effort is to catch the spirit of Christ, not merely to turn his precepts into laws or constitutions or treaties. We can hardly acquiesce, however, in anything other than the spirit of adventure. In England, the Foreign

Minister of a Labor Cabinet was questioned as to his policy. "We shall try to follow the Golden Rule," he said; whereupon a sturdy representative of the old order exclaimed, "Then God help us." And the answer came back, in a flash, "We think He will."

Chapter XI: Four Biographies

EFORE passing from Christ's teaching to his works of love and mercy, we should expect, possibly, some outline in general chronological order of the story of his life. At once we find that it is impossible to determine with any accuracy the exact course of events, nor can we even be sure of the length of Christ's public ministry.

This is because, strictly speaking, none of the scriptural accounts is a *Life of Christ;* they are all studies of his ministry, memorabilia, not biographical data carefully chronicled and arranged; collections of anecdotes about him, his words, and his works, one suggesting another by similarity or contrast of ideas. That makes them all the more vivid and interesting. One need never regret that the four men who wrote the story give it, each in his own way and for his own purpose. Each record has life, freshness, beauty, which a carefully arranged story trying to harmonize all differences and combine varied impressions would utterly lack.

It is now the generally accepted theory that the first written gospel is that which we know as the

Gospel according to St. Mark. It sketches with swift but sure touch the story of the ministry from its beginning, beyond the Jordan, when John came preaching the baptism of repentance. Tradition says that it is a written record of the oral teaching of the Apostle Peter, and the trend of recent criticism enthusiastically supports this tradition.

John Mark, a young man at whose own home the disciples met after the resurrection, went out as a companion of Paul and Barnabas on their first missionary journey. There was some unfortunate disagreement, and Mark left. Paul and Barnabas had a sharp argument over his conduct and ended each by going his own way. Reliable tradition tells us that eventually Mark joined Peter. It is good to know positively that in the end he and Paul came together again and that he was a comfort to the latter in his imprisonment. In the intervening years, however, the young man is said to have traveled with Peter.

One can easily picture Peter telling his story of the Master's life. Of course, he did not tell it consecutively. He said something here, something there, as the purpose of his discourse required; now the account of his own call; now one or another of the marvelous things he had seen; now one of the Lord's own stories; or, again, he swiftly sketched some warning of the impending tragedy; now there were fuller accounts of the suffering and the death. It is all singularly alive. One thing suggests another, as suited to the didactic purpose of the narrative, and it is told at once; perhaps three or four events are brought together because of common characteristics. The story moves with dramatic tenseness. "Anon" they tell Christ of a sick friend; "immediately" he comes here or goes there; "at once" he departs again; "quickly" some news spreads; "straightway" he gives orders to his disciples. Here we see the young man who "came running"; there, also, "the people came running together" to look at the man who had just been cured. All is swift movement and there is hardly an unnecessary word. Unfortunately the story of the resurrection, as Peter originally told it, has been lost, and the present ending of the Gospel has been added as a hurried sketch to take its place.

Whether the story is Peter's or not, it sounds like his; especially as it never spares him. It is this gospel which tells most about his boastfulness; which shows him impulsively offering advice to his Master, which tells how quick he was to talk, without stopping always to make sure that he had anything to say, which gives the language of the Master's rebuke, so sharp and severe, "Get behind me, Satan", which makes the account of his cowardice at the end doubly tragic because it tells how he heard the cock crow twice (not once), and how he had blundered on to his third denial before the second crowing recalled him to himself; which then tells of his bitter tears of penitence.

If it was not Mark who took down the story from the apostle's lips, at any rate it must have been repeated often until its words were familiar to many, and some one put it into writing almost word for word as it was spoken. There is little effort at exact chronology, though the story moves easily on its logical way. Now and then, indeed, there is a note which turns the tale back upon itself and proves that for the most part the writer's intention is to bring together incidents of a like character, without following precisely the time order of the events. It is "a necklace of pearls of which the string has been broken."

One personal note in the account of the betrayal and arrest (written into the narrative as an artist would paint his own face or the face of some one of his patron's family in an obscure figure in a picture) is a bit of reminiscence that sheds its ray of reliability on the book, and has been taken as an indication of John Mark's authorship. It is in the night of the seizure of Christ. In the crowd "a certain young man, having a linen cloth cast about his naked body"—possibly the young son of the house where the supper was held, who sprang out of bed and ran out after the Master and his disciples—was caught in the rush when the servants of the high priest made the arrest, and pulling himself free "left the linen cloth and fled from them naked."

St. Mark's is the earliest of our written Gospels. St. Matthew's Gospel uses this same Mark narrative. Its purpose is to give the Lord's teaching, rather than to describe his deeds. It is the general critical belief that the so-called *Logia,* or *Sayings of Jesus,* which we have in Matthew, come from a second document, used by Luke as well as by the editor of the first Gospel. So Matthew has the collection of most of the Lord's discourses, the parables of the kingdom, the predictions of the judgment, the denunciations of the Pharisees, the many addresses combined in what is called the Sermon on the Mount. Whoever wrote Matthew's Gospel took these and added enough of the story from the original used in St. Mark to tie the whole together. The book reads like a "lectionary"; it has a stateliness of movement which suggests that the various chapters may have taken their present form as they were read in the services at which the first Christians gathered for worship. There is a special effort to show how Jewish prophecy was fulfilled in Jesus; in particular throughout the birth narratives. He is always depicted as the Jewish Messiah, the Son of David. So careful is the author in writing for the Jews that, whereas Mark reports the Lord as going to the coasts, or borders, of Phoenicia, Matthew makes the Canaanite woman "come out of those parts" to meet him and ask his aid.

The third Gospel, which we call St. Luke's, is the "literary Gospel"; that is, it is drawn from many sources, including the original St. Mark and the second document used in St. Matthew and is carefully written, with clear connections, but having continuity of ideas rather than of time. It is rich in early stories of the birth and childhood. These, it should be noted, do not fall within the scope of the Mark Gospel, which is a narrative of the public ministry only. Many instances could be given of its literary style. Even the words which Mary and Zacharias and Simeon are quoted as using, in giving voice to their deep emotions, have a smoothness and grace which may indicate that they have been carefully revised. On the other hand, it may be that they naturally take a poetical form, because in each case the speaker's thought was saturated with the language of the Old Testament and found utterance in words that reflect the majestic and rhythmic beauty of the old writings.

This third Gospel is the story of Christ for the

Gentile world, as the Gospel according to St. Matthew is for the Jews. The author was a companion of the Apostle Paul, and we are not surprised, therefore, to find that in this Gospel "there is tenderness, sympathy for the poor, a burning zeal against those who use riches ill and oppress or neglect the poor, admiration for Zacchæus who dares a princely act of generous restitution. There is honor for women. There is an insistence on the possibility of forgiveness of sins, with which is associated a deep sense of the weakness and ignorance of man, of the magnanimity of God, of the joy of penitence. The bounds of the Gospel widen; to Samaritans, to all the nations beginning from Jerusalem." St. Luke shows Jesus in his gentleness and all-embracing love. It has been said that Luke seems to report the actual words and deeds of Christ which give the background of fact on which Paul paints his portrait of the Lord's character. You see Christ here as doing and saying, for example, that which corresponds to the Christ-love of the famous chapter on Charity in Paul's Epistle to the Corinthians. It all indicates the acquaintance of the "Apostle to the Gentiles" with the facts recorded in the "Gentile Gospel," and since Paul's epistles are now recognized as unquestionably authentic, the third Gospel has new historic significance.

We shall see, later, that all three of these narratives convey the same general impression of Jesus. Essentially, it is not in conflict with the ideas afterward more clearly presented in the book we call the Gospel according to St. John. Exactly the same view is expounded in the letters written by the Apostle Paul, and it should be remembered that some of these are among the earliest of the New Testament writings. The earlier Gospels, however, while they contain the ideas, do not present them so sharply and distinctly. The ideas are present in the "synoptic" Gospels; the Lord is there represented as making divine claims; but there is no attempt to show how faith grew, nor to accommodate the story to meet later thought; while in St. John all is clear as crystal.

That need not puzzle us. The purpose of Christ's coming was to live a perfectly human life and to enter upon truly human relations, and only slowly did the mystery of his being impress itself upon his companions. They always felt much more than they expressed at the time, and these early Gospels—they are now universally admitted to be of very early date—give an account of the events as written in the first century, but told orally, from the beginning, by eyewitnesses who were still living in the awe and wonder of their experience but had not yet found it necessary to search for words in which they could give a satisfactory explanation of the mystery. These witnesses tell exactly what was done and said and felt at the time of the events, and tell only that, without much comment.

Yet these are actually the Gospels that tell of the claim of Jesus to have been endowed with authority from the Father as the judge of men. It is here that we read of his declaration that he was coming again for a great assize, when he would summon all men before him. Who but a crazy fanatic could have made such a claim, unless he knew whereof he spoke and unless his claim was really true?

It is in these Gospels that we read of the healing of the paralytic and of the claim of Jesus to exercise authority on earth to forgive sins. Here, also, we hear him telling Simon Peter that the declaration of faith he made could have been learned only from "my Father which is in heaven." Here are recorded the words in which he said that "no man knoweth the Father, but the Son, and he to whom the Son willeth to reveal him." Here we begin to see what being the Messiah meant to Jesus. We are plunged as deep into mystery as in any of the later writings as we trace his thought and find him speaking of giving his life "a ransom for many." We feel the mystery grow, as the Gospels describe the Last

Supper and we hear him speak of his body broken and his blood shed, "for you and for many, for the remission of sins."

There can be no doubt that these early Gospels give a substantially accurate record of the effect which the actions and bearing, as well as the teaching, of Jesus had on his companions. They did not at once solve the riddle; but what is written here is what these men said about their Master from the very first, and what they say shows him as standing in some unique relation to God and men, claiming unmeasured authority over them and receiving from them unquestioned recognition of that authority.

What we call the Gospel according to St. John is an interpretation rather than a history. Early tradition declared it to be the work of the apostle and recognized its supplementary character. Naturally, if it was so written, its story would be told just as we find that it actually is given: omitting parts of the ministry of which the other Gospels tell; explaining sometimes what they record briefly and adding comment and interpretation; making alterations where their records had been found unintelligible; referring only in passing to incidents already told in detail elsewhere; often writing so as to be understood only by those familiar with the earlier narrative; assuming, apparently, their existence and a widespread knowledge of their contents.

Tradition declares that in this way, well toward the end of the first century, John told the Lord's story afresh, with the other Gospels before him, to comfort his converts in their perplexity. His was the only living voice that could tell of the wonderful days in Judea and Galilee. All the other companions of the Lord were gone. Long before this, it had been supposed, Jesus would have returned in glory; had he not said that John would tarry till he came? But time passed and John was growing old and feeble; still the Lord delayed his coming. These friends of John began to see that they had been mistaken in their expectations. No, the Lord had never said that John was to tarry till he came; it was only, "If I will that he tarry, what is that to you?"

What the writer of the Gospel seeks to do is, not only to clear up such misunderstandings, but also to correct apparent discrepancies in the earlier Gospels and especially to supply a fuller account of the Lord's work in Judea, since their narratives had related almost exclusively the Galilean ministry. In particular, he would begin with a statement of their fully reasoned faith, and then in telling his story show how this faith had issued out of their experience.

The authenticity of the Gospel as being the work of the Apostle John has been attacked repeatedly. Whether it would have been so persistently attacked were it not that its supernatural teaching is so sharp, may be doubted. At the same time, it ought in fairness to be said that doubts have arisen, not simply because of the supernatural doctrine of this Gospel, but because it seems, at first, to give a picture of Christ quite unlike the other three; its record of his utterances quotes him in language so dissimilar to theirs; its whole thought is so different, as compared with the rugged simplicity of earlier evangelists; it seems to move in another sphere and live in another atmosphere.

Of late, however, it has come to be felt that "the evidence connecting the Gospel in some way with St. John is irresistible." It seems to tell his story and reflect his mind, and might well be the work of one standing in the same relation to St. John as that of St. Mark to St. Peter. Lord Charnwood, the English biographer of Lincoln and an historical student of no mean ability, has applied to this Gospel the critical methods with the use of which he is so familiar, and has considered the whole problem of the authorship of the Gospel with the robust common sense of a layman, untrammeled by theological presuppositions and unprejudiced by dogmatic theories or too fine critical distinctions. He comes to the conclusion that "while there is some uncertainty (which may always remain) as to the historical authority to be attached to this Gospel in some details, the extent of that uncertainty is much reduced when we consider more clearly the writer's purpose and method. Several considerations make us regard [the addresses at the Last Supper] as the most certainly trustworthy and most important part of the Gospel." They give "a fresh and living portrayal" of Jesus.

This does not necessarily imply that St. John actually composed the book, and "the theory that it is the work of one of his pupils who records what he had heard from the apostle is quite a natural supposition; but it remains a natural explanation, only if when given to the early church it was known to have substantially St. John's authority behind it."

"Make of it what we may," says Lord Charnwood, "Jesus Christ of Nazareth did think and did speak as according to St. John he thought and spoke concerning his Father, himself, his followers, and that Spirit of his which should abide with them forever." It will be important to remember this when we come finally to a discussion of Christ's miracles and of his divine claims.

And to one who has read much of the speculations of historical critics who are also theologians this view of a candid layman, careful never to overstate his case, is refreshing in its clarity and sound sense. We owe much to historical criticism. Just as it won the victory for the Old Testament by showing its naturalness of method, frankly admitting its use of myth and legend, and interpreting its writings as Oriental in their imaginative power, while at the same time vitalizing the book by bringing out so vividly the prophetic writings—so, now, through it we find a similar "humanizing" of the New Testament. The Gospels may no longer be attributed to the apostles as their own composition, but when we learn how the compilers use the apostolic story in editing their work, we discover the whole narrative as much more interesting and "alive." The overrefinement of criticism need not blind us to its real value. Scholars may be too ready to prune away what conflicts with some special theory or to discover literary purposes alien to the mind of the apostles' time; yet in the main they have made the Gospel record more vivid and authoritative.

Chapter XII: The Testimony of Eyewitnesses

EAD for the first time, the story of Christ's life would be extraordinarily interesting. It could not fail to arouse attention and to impress us with its freshness and naturalness. Many questions would trouble the reader, of course, because of its supernatural elements; for we do not move easily into a world of miracle. Apart from that, however, for us of today the reading is handicapped by an embarrassing remembrance of agelong controversies over the meaning of the story, by accustomed habits of thought, by conventional ideas and inherited misunderstandings.

If we could put away all preconceptions and read the story straight through, we should find that it presents a wonderfully vivid picture. It is difficult to see how such a reading could fail to clear away many doubts as to the actual beliefs of the writers, the substantial harmony of the different accounts, and the strong sense of reality which pervades the whole history.

It cannot be fiction. Nobody ever wrote fiction in this way. Dispute as we may about questions of authorship, the evidence that the narratives have been told by eyewitnesses is so strong as to increase this assurance of their truth and at the same time to stir up in us a deep sense of reverence. The books may be compilations from several sources, but they bear clear evidence that the original sources were the actual records of those who had themselves seen and heard.

This is true of all four of the Gospels. Who but an eyewitness could tell of how an eager youth "came running to Jesus," kneeling to him and asking what he must do to inherit eternal life? No one in that simple literary age could have invented such a scene. Who but some one who honestly wrote exactly what he saw would dare to say (remembering what these men had come to believe about their Master) that on one occasion, when the Pharisees put their Sabbath laws above all human pity, Jesus "looked about on them with anger"? Who but one who had looked into his eyes could have described his ways with children? Who but a friend watching him closely and lovingly could have noticed how, as he "sat over against the treasury," he observed the poor bringing their offerings? Surely, too, it is an eyewitness who tells how "he was grieved for the hardness of their hearts," when the Pharisees were so full of murderous thoughts because he had healed, on the Sabbath day, the man with the withered hand. It was one who was himself present who declared that Jesus "sighed deeply" when the Pharisees, although they knew of his works, still asked for "a sign."

It may not be easy to accept the accounts of his miracles, but surely it is even harder to think the whole story an invention which tells how when the blind man was brought to him, "he took him by the hand, and led him out of town"; how "he put his fingers again upon his eyes, and made him look up." Quite close to him must have been the man who told of the day when the crowd pressed about him and a poor woman crept up and "touched the hem of his garment" and he "knew in himself that virtue (or power) had gone out of him."

It must have been one such as Peter who described the company as "they were in the way, going up to Jerusalem, and Jesus went before them"—eager, determined, with set purpose to do the right thing, even though it were the hard thing—"and they were amazed, and as they followed him they were afraid."

These are from the record of Mark, but there is the same note in the other Gospels. Think of Luke's account of the woman who slipped through the crowd, came into Simon's house, and—careless of the crowd, with utter lack of self-consciousness, anxious only to show her gratitude—broke her box of ointment, anointed the Master's feet, washed them with her tears, and wiped them with her hair. One can see Simon, untouched, cold, critical, disapproving, plainly annoyed at the unseemliness of such a "scene" in his own home. And then Jesus said unto him, "Simon, I have something to say to you." Then—note this and ask if it is pure invention—Jesus "turned to the woman"—looked first at Simon and then down at the penitent—and the parable followed with its moral of the largeness of pardon and blessing for those who love much. You see the Master's response to the appeal of moral weakness, but you are also let into the mind of the appalled and unsympathetic Pharisee who stood silently passing judgment on Christ's claims.

Could anyone have told, unless he had been present, of the four men who brought their paralytic friend to Jesus and, when the crowd about the entrance prevented their going into the house, carried him on his litter up the outside stairs and out to the roof overhanging the balcony of the inner court, to let him down among the amazed people pressing about Christ? The novelist who could in that day write fiction in this vivid fashion, and paint a picture in a paragraph, is yet to be found.

Must it not have been one of the apostles who first told the story, which Luke repeats, of how the Lord's Prayer was given? "It came to pass, as he was praying in a certain place, that they said, Lord, teach us to pray"—as if when they came upon him at his devotions they realized for the first time what prayer really could be and wanted to know the secret of such worship. Again, one actually sees "the woman who had a spirit of infirmity eighteen years, and was bowed together and could in no wise lift up herself." One understands the other woman who had "spent all her living upon physicians" and was in no way improved in health, but only the worse for all their experiments. And then there is that "certain blind man who sat by the wayside begging, and hearing the multitude passing by, asked what it meant." You actually have him before you; you look at him as he sits there, puzzled by the movement of the crowd, not able to see, but trying to guess what it is all about, finally clutching at the garment of one of the men in the crowd to ask.

There are touches, also, which clearly come from one who was present, when Luke notes how jealously the Pharisees "watched him" for some fresh occasion of complaint. You hear the subdued and angry muttering when "the Pharisees and scribes murmured, saying, This man receiveth sinners and eateth with them." Certainly Luke had gathered his facts from the records of eyewitnesses. In every chapter there is evidence of it.

Apart from the fact that the three Gospels give a consistent picture of Christ, which could never have been one man's invention, much less the simultaneous invention of several authors, there is the drawing of other characters; notably that of Peter, who appears often in each of the Gospels, and is always and everywhere the same. The portrait is an etching and there is no line drawn by any of the three artists which is not true to the life.

Nor is St. John's story only the meditative contemplation of one who is always transmuting the Lord's words into the language of the mystic, or of one adapting them to the thought of a later period. Hardly. Here is a man who remembered so vividly his first introduction to Jesus that he could stop to say, "It was just ten o'clock in the morning," who remembered also how "Jesus turned and looked at them" when they followed.

Whatever may be the explanation of the turning of water into wine, something happened at Cana and John was there to see it; he never wove into an allegory this charming story and then gave the illusion of naturalness to the tale by telling how Mary said to the servants, "Whatsoever he tells you to do, do it." Although the story of the woman taken in adultery is a misplaced fragment of the Gospel, no one merely imagined that "Jesus stooped and wrote on the ground" before he looked up and told those who themselves were without sin to cast stones at the trembling offender they had dragged into his presence. Some have supposed the story to belong to St. Luke rather than to St. John, but it bears marks quite as common to the fourth Gospel, where it was probably slipped into the wrong place in the manuscript.

Is it difficult to believe that Lazarus was actually raised from death? Well, is it easy to believe that the story is one of many inventions? Who in those days ever told in that way about something that was but a figment of the imagination? "Mary ran to meet him." "Oh, Master, if you had only been here." Her weeping. The hysterical wailing of the neighbors. The groaning sigh of Jesus. His own tears. Unpleasant as the words are, what glaring evidence of the genuineness of the narrative we have in Martha's protest that decay must already have set in on the body four days buried.

Who but the beloved disciple could have told in just the way this Gospel tells it the story of the Last Supper, with the washing of the feet, Peter's indignant remonstrance, the question asked by the disciple who reclined next to the Master and leaned over on his breast?

And the crucifixion: What did the evangelist mean when he told of the water and the blood that gushed out of the Lord's body at the thrust of the soldier's spear? Was it evidence of the sudden rupture of the heart, and is that the explanation of the sharp, loud, terrible cry of anguish uttered a few moments before death? Can anyone have told of the incident save the man whose memory was forever haunted by it, and to whom afterward it seemed that just then, in those dark and awful hours, his faith returned and "he saw and believed"?

And the resurrection: He and Peter running to the tomb; he outrunning Peter (and in his old age recalling it with a bit of pardonable pride), though not daring to go in; Peter rushing forward impulsively; he following; both seeing the graveclothes lying in perfect order, the napkin that was about his head fallen a little aside by itself; no confusion, no signs of any disturbance or defiling of the tomb; every indication that the body had simply evanished out of the clothes, leaving them fallen flat on the slab. And again: "he saw and believed."

No: the Gospels do not give us chronological history; they may occasionally err as to minor details; they may each have been written to support a particular view; they are probably only the work of those who came after the apostles; but their story has apostolic authority back of it. When we read, we are reading what had actually been told by those whose eyes had gazed upon, whose hands had handled the Word of Life. They are the real reminiscences of men whose loving recollections remind them ever of other facts, which they at once relate, as if to say, "Speaking of that, I am reminded"; not bare history, but wonderful biography.

Chapter XIII: Three Crowded Years

IT IS far better to have biographies such as these than to have a complete record of the life of the Lord, told with chronological exactness; but for that very reason told, probably, with personal impressions lost, as well as contradictions swept away.

Yet we should like to know more of the exact record. How long did Jesus teach, a year and a half, or three years? Just when did this or that happen, or in what circumstances was such and such teaching given? If we could only know, we think we should understand better what the teaching means. One may be permitted to doubt it.

The difficulty of combining all the Gospels into a chronological harmony arises from the fact that John's Gospel tells fully the story of the ministry in Judea, while the others tell more about the work and teaching in Galilee. The almost impossible task of fitting both together is further increased by uncertainty as to the "feast of the Jews" which Jesus attended on the occasion of the healing of the impotent man at the pool of Bethesda. What feast was it—the Passover? If

John had only been more definite in telling about this feast, many a problem in harmonizing the Gospels would have been solved. Perhaps, after all, he cared more for vividness than for mechanical accuracy. Other difficulties spring out of John's record of the passion and death, but plain common sense would not assume contradictions here; it may be taken for granted that fuller knowledge would clear up apparent discrepancies. Whether, for example, the Last Supper which Christ celebrated with his apostles was actually the Jewish Passover Supper, or was a preliminary rite, the so-called "Sanctification" of the Passover, held the night before, we shall probably never know.

Not only are there difficulties in reconciling St. John's and the other three (or synoptic) Gospels, but there are further differences in these three narratives. This is due to the fact that these Gospels represent, as we have seen, the result of the "editing" of a great mass of material—narratives taken down from the lips of eyewitnesses and long in circulation; some of them broken up into sections, without chronological order. The writers of the Gospels "lift" these narratives and put them into their own record, often as illustrating something in immediate connection with the story they themselves are telling. Sometimes there are evidences of so scrupulous a regard for literal reproduction that these sections, lifted and placed in the new narrative, appear with their original introductory sentences unchanged.

All of which means that the effort to fix certainly a chronological order is bound to fail; but it indicates, nevertheless, several other interesting facts: *e.g.,* that differences hard to compose are not necessarily contradictory, but are evidence of an unwillingness to shade away variations; or, again, that we have here a very different picture of the way in which the scriptures were written than that which makes the writers, not authors or editors, but amanuenses of God! Why, if that were the case, should there be verbal differences so impossible to explain?

If we knew more of the order of events, we should see how great crises arose in the Lord's ministry, how he met them, and how his plans were modified in accommodation to new conditions. While we cannot, with reasonable certainty, get such an approximately accurate survey, assuming that the uncertain "feast of the Jews" mentioned by St. John was the Passover, the public ministry of Jesus was something over three years in extent. Briefly, it would then be sketched as follows.

After the marriage in Cana of Galilee, Jesus and his disciples went up to Jerusalem to the

Passover festival. While there, according to St. John, he cleansed the temple. During this visit, also, Nicodemus came for his private interview by night. About this time, John the Forerunner was arrested. This event seems to have determined Jesus to leave Judea and to go into Galilee, where his doctrine was likely to receive a readier hearing. On the way, he met the woman of Samaria at the well, and many of the Samaritans accepted him. He taught in Galilee, healed the son of the nobleman at Capernaum, spoke in the synagogue in Nazareth, and when rejected by his own home people took up his residence in Capernaum. Here we have the record of more teaching and of an extensive work of healing. Here also the mother of Peter's wife was healed, and here Peter and some of the others received a more definite call. Among them was Matthew, also called Levi, a customs collector.

Now comes, following such a supposed chronology, the second Passover, with the second attempt to win Jerusalem. It is a failure, despite the healing at the Bethesda pool. It is interesting to note the reason for this failure. Jesus would not accommodate himself to the hard Sabbatarian views of the Pharisees. No wonder. They had "blue laws" which only ecclesiastical specialists ever fully catalogued. Solemn denunciations of trifles such as plucking ears of corn and rubbing them in the hands on a Sabbath journey—think of it! Reaping was forbidden Sabbath work, and this could be called reaping. Similarly, ploughing was forbidden; digging was ploughing; dragging anything over the ground in such a way as to make a rut was digging, and therefore punishable. The spirit of love was so lost that a sick man just cured must not walk home on the Sabbath carrying the pallet on which he had been resting. There was a catalogue of thirty-nine offenses punishable by death, if done deliberately, and expiated by an offering for sin, if committed inadvertently. Orthodoxy became bigotry. That which was made for man's blessing was turned into his despair.

One may wonder that Jesus thought it necessary persistently to run counter to such prejudices, but it should be remembered that this severe Sabbatarianism was absolutely and utterly opposed to the very core of his teaching. It made God an irritating ruler, jealous for the observance of a lot of little legalities; it made of man a worried slave, fearful of passing across the line of strict observance and suffering the prescribed consequences; while Jesus made God a loving Father, looking for loving service.

It was after this visit to Jerusalem and the return to Galilee that the fame of Jesus spread abroad and he performed many cures, one said to be a raising from death, when he restored to the widow of Nain the boy whose body she was following to the burial. Finally, retiring to the mountain side, after a night of prayer he chose the Twelve. Here came also the delivery of a teaching address included in the Sermon on the Mount. Shortly afterward a delegation from John visited him, seeking assurance for their master (now in prison) that he had made no mistake in recognizing Jesus as the Messiah. This was Christ's answer: Go and show John again the things you hear and see. Tell him that the blind receive their sight, that the lame walk. Tell him how the lepers are cleansed, how the deaf hear. Tell him that the dead are raised. Tell him that the poor are hearing the good news. Happy are they who find in me no occasion of complaint.

There followed, then, a long series of miracles of healing; another circuit of Galilee, when many of the parables were given; the raising of the daughter of Jairus; the death of John; another rejection by his home people. "Who is this man?" they ask. "Is he not the carpenter, the son of Mary? Are not his brothers and sisters here with us? Whence came to him any special wisdom? How can he claim to do great works?"

It is worthy of brief note that in St. Mark's Gospel Christ is spoken of as "the carpenter, the son of Mary," in St. Matthew's as "the carpenter's son." Why? Is it because St. Matthew records the story of the miraculous birth and may safely use the actual language of the Nazareth people, while St. Mark, who begins with the public ministry and therefore has not told anything about the birth, for that reason modifies the words? In St. Luke's Gospel, he is called by others "the son of Joseph." Are the words recorded without comment or explanation, because in this Gospel also the truth has already been safeguarded?

After this, the action moves still more swiftly. A third circuit of Galilee is the occasion for sending out the newly appointed apostles "to preach the Kingdom of God and to heal the sick." On their return he crossed the lake with them, and there fed the five thousand. It is on this occasion that the story is told of his walking on the water. St. John follows the account of the feeding of the multitude with the discourse in the synagogue at Capernaum on the Bread of Life— "the bread which cometh down from heaven, and giveth life to the world."

Strangely enough, after this miracle the popularity of Jesus began to wane. And yet it is not so strange. He who knew the heart of man saw that the crowd had followed him out of curiosity and that they wanted a Messiah who would satisfy the national expectations. They "labored for the food which is perishable"; they "sought him because they had eaten of the loaves and were full"; and they were impatient of his talk about life-giving "bread from heaven."

It was another crisis in his career. The crowd was leaving him—what about the twelve? Would they also go away? We know that it was the beginning of the downfall of Judas. Not so with the others. Peter, always impulsive, sometimes foolish, but never anything but loyal in all his weakness, was quick to voice the thought of the rest as well as his own convictions, and testified to his faith in words which those who cannot fully accept Christianity today would do well to consider: "Lord, to whom shall we go? Thou hast the words of eternal life, and we believe and are sure that thou art the Christ, the Son of the Living God."

They had expected much and had expected it at once; but now they are puzzled and disappointed. The foundations seem to be slipping. But though they do not understand, they feel that they cannot have been mistaken. There can be no surer light than they have had, no higher revelation.

There are many practical people today who cannot think things out very clearly, and who are not able to express what they do think. They hold fast their faith, because, whether they understand or not, they feel that in the Christian religion the last possible word has been spoken about God and his world, and there can be no revelation beyond it. Give it up? Romanes lost his faith in a personal God, though afterward he recovered it, and the words in which he expressed his sense of loss are full of tragic intensity: "When I think, as think I must, of the hallowed glory of that creed which once was mine, and the lonely mystery of existence as I now find it—at such times it will ever be impossible for me to avoid the sharpest pang of which my nature is susceptible."

Give up the Christian faith, and what can take its place? Doubtless it is hard to adjust new ideas to the older truths. Unquestionably there are difficulties. But, after all, is it not this or nothing?

Now we come to the third Passover: More miracles; more objections from the Pharisees to his infractions of the ceremonial law, such as eating without observance of the ritual washing of the hands; then his warnings against "the leaven of the Pharisees," when the apostles must have sorely tempted his patience by their stupid misunderstanding of his words; other parables; a final departure from Galilee, to go up to the Feast of Tabernacles.

It is before this journey that the momentous question is asked of Peter: "Who say ye that I am?" When Peter's answer declared his growing faith, Jesus began to give them some warnings of his approaching passion, and told how he was to be rejected and killed—"and the third day rise again." It was then that Peter (whose avowal of faith had just been praised) presumed to "rebuke" the Master, "That be far from thee, Lord; this shall not be unto thee"—presumption which met with a response so severe as to indicate the sharpness of temptation which the Master felt in its suggestion of possible compromise and escape.

Just before this had come the mysterious transfiguration on the mountain; just after came the mission of the seventy disciples, who were then sent out on a journey such as the twelve had already undertaken.

And then, in quick succession: the return of the seventy; a visit to Mary and Martha; parables such as that of the Good Samaritan; further teaching in the temple during the feast days; an attempt of the Jews to stone him to death; the Feast of the Dedication, after which he retired beyond the Jordan; still more teaching; more miracles, including the raising of Lazarus.

And now, at last, the drama draws to its close. He "set his face steadfastly to go to Jerusalem," foretelling again his death and resurrection, and six days before the Passover he arrived at Simon's house in Bethany. The order of the rest of the story is more plain. We shall leave the history, therefore, to go back to the works of the Master.

Chapter XIV: The Good Physician

ESUS CHRIST was not only the Great Teacher; he was the Good Physician. Even those who stumble at other miracles have reached the point of accepting the accounts of his healing mission, however they may explain the facts. Indeed, it could hardly be otherwise, if we are to preserve any living portrait of Christ; for the records of his gracious deeds run so closely through the gospel narrative that they are like threads woven in the cloth which cannot be cut away without destroying the garment.

The picture is clear. Jesus went about the towns and villages and through the countryside of Galilee restoring into harmony with the beautiful world about him the sin-sick souls and disease-laden bodies of those who came to him for help. It was indeed a beautiful land then, though now Turkish rule has desolated it and its villages are filthy to a degree unimaginable in our Lord's day and under the sanitary regulations of the Mosaic law. To most of those who came to see him, Jesus was first known as the "Healer."

And many came, attracted by his fame. The

demands upon his skill spread like wildfire. Everywhere the sick came with their calls upon his sympathy and vitality. His patients were of all classes, all disorders, all shades of faith, all degrees of gratitude and ingratitude. They crowded upon him till he hardly had time to eat or to sleep.

Although his pity forbade him to refuse aid to those who crowded about him, in general he was reluctant to press overmuch his healing powers. He "crossed to the other side" of the lake to avoid the patients who pursued him. He healed because of his compassion; but his real purpose was to teach, and so he escaped as often as possible, going apart into lonely places to pray, seeking solitude for his disciples as well as for himself. "Come ye yourselves apart, and rest awhile."

It was not that he wished to restrain his gifts, though there may have been such a natural feeling of self-protection, inasmuch as we read that "virtue (power) went out of him" at the healing touch. His real reason was that had he allowed himself to become merely a "miracle man," the whole purpose of his life would have been frustrated and it would have been impossible to keep alive his own contacts with the Father or to deepen the communion with his disciples. His first task was to teach them and gradually to bring them into such absorption in his person and purpose that they could safely be left to carry on the spiritual work for which he had chosen them. While we cannot make the miracles other than an integral part of his ministry, yet he himself did not lay much stress upon them. He absolutely refused to perform any work save as he was moved thereto by the spirit of mercy. The Pharisees were always demanding of him "a sign"; even Herod hoped, on one occasion, to see some miracle wrought by him, but that was not the way he desired to win adherence.

There is something more important than bodily health—health of spirit—and we do well to remember that Jesus plainly implied this in the economy he exercised in the use of his healing gifts. The purpose of the Christian religion is not to make life easier, but to make men brave to endure. Faith is not given that all pain may be removed and perfect peace secured; its fruit is the patient bearing of suffering. Probably the fact of pain—sin, suffering, sorrow—is the outstanding obstacle to faith in a loving God. Jesus gave no solution of the problem. But he did show how to face suffering and sorrow. On occasion also, he lifted the burden for some. His followers must be exercising the same ministry of mercy; but they, too, should remember that there are deeper wants than the need for physical comfort, bodily health, and happiness; and even in helpful service, which is the fruit of Christian love, they should seek to satisfy the real hungers of the human heart.

The effect of mind upon matter has always been a mystery. Men talk much about it; but no one understands it, not even men of science. And the mind itself is a mystery. A diseased mind puzzles the best of physicians. They, too, may talk much about the mystery; but their talking does not explain it. They may tell us about dual personalities and the subliminal self, about various "complexes" and neurasthenic delusions; and yet the mystery remains.

In Christ's day the general belief was that mental and even bodily diseases were to be ascribed to malignant spirits. Nowadays we talk of epilepsy, feeble-mindedness, insanity, various dementias; whereas in his day those who so suffered were said to be possessed of demons. Well, who knows but that we may come back to such a view? Popular theories come and go. Freudian psychology has its run, and then its influence wanes. Coué is the sensation of the day, and then is forgotten. The dangers of psychological treatment are recognized. A fashionable fad soon becomes unfashionable. What remains is the undoubted fact that the power of suggestion has much to do with recovery to a normal healthy life. What remains, also, is that mental health, and in particular spiritual health, has much to do with physical health.

So it has come about that many of the cures effected by Christ, once denied, are now accepted. Not accepted as miracles, of course; but, after all, that is a mere matter of language. A miracle is not a violation of law; it is something brought about in obedience to a law which we have not yet discovered.

The demon-possessed whom Christ healed were cured through the dominating power of his personality. Similar cures are effected now by those to whom God has given a similar strength of influence. Does that mean that the miracles of Christ are in no way a proof of his deity? That is not the actual case, but it is true that we have long since ceased to use them in practical argument to convince the unbeliever. They have always been something of a stumblingblock to the modern mind. As a matter of fact, also, the most orthodox theologians have long contended that Jesus did not rely upon his divine powers during his earthly life; but used human powers such as those with which we are endowed, only in his case fortified in unique degree by divine grace and in no way weakened by sin.

And what a list we have of his cures! The

man in the country of the Gergesenes whose "other self" cried out that his name was "Legion," as if a great regiment of spirits held him in possession; the blind and dumb man, suffering also from epileptic fits; the boy at the foot of the Transfiguration Mount who fell in convulsions, often tumbling into the fire or into the water; others of whom no particulars are given. How characteristic of a scene of today is the story of the man in the synagogue at Nazareth who suddenly cried out, "Let us alone; what have we to do with thee, thou Jesus of Nazareth? Art thou come to destroy us?" Was he perhaps a religious fanatic, or an epileptic, taken to public worship instead of being sent to a state hospital?

If it be objected that in accommodating himself to the ideas of the age Jesus was guilty of deceit, suppose we stop to ask what other possible course was open to him if he were to effect his cures. A medical lecture in the terms of a modern psychoanalyst would not have conveyed anything to the minds of the people of that age. He could not have told them carefully about psychiatric treatments; that would have been utterly inconsistent with his usual method. There is evidence enough that Jesus did not share in the superstitions of the theory of demoniacal possession, but had a strong sense of religious and moral values; but he necessarily accommodated himself to the thought of those about him. This was in line with his general plan. It has already been pointed out that he never told his disciples "plainly" of his own unique nature, he left them to find it out for themselves. This is in line with God's plan. The Bible does not teach science, it teaches religion. Mankind has never been relieved of the necessity of investigation and discovery and never will be. We are free spirits seeking for truth; never empty receptacles to be filled automatically.

And as has already been asked: Who knows how much of truth there may be in the doctrine of evil spirits? A generation ago, men would have laughed at our present-day psychology; a generation hence, men may laugh at what we now accept without reservations. Remembering that the accounts of the miracles of healing run through all the Gospels and cannot be wrenched out of the story, we are finally coming to seek an explanation for them. Our explanation may not be true, but at least our attitude is more sane than that of a past generation which discarded entirely the miraculous element and sought to reconstruct the life of Jesus without it—simply and solely because they declared the events recorded to be impossible.

We must go a step further when we consider Christ's other miracles of healing. Evidence of extraordinary power they certainly manifested, and it is more difficult, if not impossible, to find a satisfactory natural explanation of his healing gift. Now and then we read of sickness that seems to be associated with sin. Is it not so associated today? Why plunge into questions of sex morality to answer? So we have a striking case when the Master first declared, "Thy sins are forgiven thee," before going on to say, "Arise and walk."

Again, what a list of cures there is! The man with the withered hand; Peter's wife's mother; the woman with the issue of blood; the centurion's servant; the man born blind; the hopeless paralytic of Bethesda; the ten lepers; the blind man (or were there two?) at Jericho; the daughter of the Syro-Phoenician woman, on his only recorded trip outside the border of his own land. In some cases, he encouraged their own will power, as when at Bethesda he asked the sick man, "Do you really want to get well?" At other times, he emphasized the need of faith: "Your faith has saved you, go in peace."

When the whole record has been read, we begin to regard with suspicion any easy explanations of the power of the great healer. Grant that he exercised personality to an extraordinary extent, as other men have exercised such influence, and in the end we begin to ask, What sort of personality must his have been? How do we explain such wonderful power? The blind man, questioned so closely and badgered so vehemently by the authorities, put it bluntly when he said, "One thing I know: that whereas I was blind; now I see. Herein is a marvelous thing, that you know not whence he is, and yet he has opened my eyes." Then they cast him out. When Jesus heard that they had excommunicated him, he found him and asked, "Do you believe on the Son of God?" "Who is he, that I may believe?" And Jesus said, "You have seen him and he is now talking with you."

These are precisely the questions men ask in these days. "Whence hath this man these things? What mean these mighty works that are wrought by his hands?" No wonder that in Gennesaret they "ran through the whole district, and began to carry about on their pallets all who were sick, when they heard where he was, and wherever he entered into villages, or cities, or in the country, they put down the sick in the streets, and besought him that they might be allowed to touch if it were but the border of his garment." And no wonder, with power like his, and faith like theirs, that "as many as touched him were made whole."

Jesus never called these works miracles. They were "signs"; outward evidence of inward power. That is what his near followers felt. They said afterward that they had seen his glory and that it was the very glory of God. Once they had felt that God was far away; now they came to find, in the love and labors of Jesus, "the infinite nearness" of the Father. There were wonderful deeds which we cannot begin to explain except on such a theory as this, difficult as the theory may be. Nature's powers seemed subject to him. He walked on the water, we are told. He stilled the storm. Once, to meet a sudden need, he reddened the water into wine. On at least one occasion there was a marvelous multiplication of a small supply of food; possibly on a second occasion as well. Finally, not merely did he heal the sick; on occasion he raised the dead—the son of the widow of Nain, the daughter of Jairus, his friend Lazarus—and often afterward people told of these things with bated breath.

Are they believable? Not unless we have come by other means to the fullest faith of the Gospel—and about such faith we shall soon inquire. Even then, are they believable? Yes, unless the scientific mind refuses to move another step onward, either in faith or knowledge. There are signs that science is becoming less impregnable to the reality of the supernatural. And, after all, what is a miracle but "the supremacy of the spiritual forces of the world to an extraordinarily marked degree over the material"?

If ever there was a time when the spiritual forces of the world were seen in concentrated power, it was in the days of Christ. And if ever the miraculous might be expected to appear, it must have been then.

Chapter XV: The Wonder of his Works

IT IS the fashion in these days—when dislike of dogma seems to go to the extreme of contempt for logic—to say that the real task of one who would go to the heart of Christianity is to disentangle the story of Christ from the miraculous, to get beneath what must be regarded as later accretions to its original truth and beauty, and to seek there to find "Jesus only"—the Christ who was so good and great that he impressed himself upon the wills and hearts of men and so indelibly fixed his teaching upon their minds and consciences that it could never be effaced.

That is the Christ we want, men say; the Christ who so mastered the souls of his followers that the fire of their faith kindled in other hearts and gave to the world a new and beautiful religion, full of God and goodness, and therefore full of power. Men, they go on to say, are anxious to accept such a Christ. Many will accept him, if we will only let them do so, without asking of them what they cannot give—acceptance of certain doctrines about him, legendary accounts of his birth, doubtful tales of his miracle-working power, an impossible story of his bodily resurrection.

For this is an ordered world, under the reign of law, in which experience teaches us that there is nothing arbitrary nor disconnected. Many things which in other times would have been regarded as miraculous interventions upon the customary order are now accounted for in a natural way. We cannot but regard with suspicion, therefore, all accounts of events supposed to have been brought about by special and extraordinary acts of God.

The story of Christ, so we are told, was written by men who were on the lookout for extraordinary interpositions of divine power. It was quite natural, therefore, that the accounts should be full of marvels. Remembered acts of his came to be exaggerated (unconsciously, of course, and without unworthy motive) until they finally took on a miraculous character and the simple Gospel became encrusted with superstitious fancies. Other acts now quite easily explained on natural lines appeared to the apostles as mighty wonders. For them, the process was inevitable; but for us, instead of bringing certitude and conviction, the intrusion of the miraculous is a hindrance to faith. Miracles simply do not happen and we cannot believe that they ever have happened.

Has it not been apparent, however, as we have followed the Gospel story, that it is absolutely impossible to eliminate the miraculous and the supernatural from the story of Jesus Christ? The narrative of St. Mark abounds in tales of healing and command over evil spirits; yet modern critics no longer regard this as evidence of remoteness from the facts. We cannot disentangle the "mighty works" and the "wonderful words." Can, then, the miraculous and supernatural coloring be justified, and if so to what degree?

Two things should be said at the outset. In the first place, as we have just seen, there is today a frank acknowledgment of the reasonableness of some modern explanations of the miracles, although at the same time it is clear that these explanations are not satisfactory in the case of all of the recorded miracles. In the second place, let it be repeated that belief in Christ is not based upon the miraculous, although one who has reached full faith in him by other roads may indeed find the manifested presence and power of the supernatural a further buttress to belief.

Jesus himself minimized the importance of his miraculous works. It always disappointed him to find that people came to him primarily as a healer. It made him feel how few there were who really cared for the good news he brought or for the kingdom he meant to establish. "Except you see signs and wonders you will not believe." If he healed, it was not because he consented to give the signs they desired, but because he could not resist human need. "Sir, come down ere my child die," cried the Capernaum nobleman, and his pity responded at once.

Faith does not come because of "signs." The Christian faith must be the result of an experience for us such as the apostles had in their life with Christ. We must live close enough to Christ and long enough with him to know him for what he is. Living with him, we find that his earthly life was a supernatural, creative element within the old world of sin and death and therefore a miraculous intervention upon the natural development of history and life. Miracle in that case becomes a reasonable accomplishment of such an intervention of God. The character of Christ and his deliberate methods with his disciples prove him to be what he claimed to be, the Unique Son of God—or else a crazy, deluded fanatic or a deliberate and blasphemous deceiver. If he was what he claimed to be, then we have the very circumstances in which, if ever, we may look for extraordinary departures from the customary natural order; unless, indeed, it be impossible to believe that there can be any departure, at any time or in any conditions, from an order of nature which we are obliged to regard as self-closed and complete;

unless, in other words, we also take our stand on the declaration that miracles never have happened, never will happen, and never can happen. Is that true?

It will help us to answer this question if we first ask, "What is a miracle?" Take this definition from Dr. Headlam: "A miracle means really the supremacy of the spiritual forces of the world to an extraordinarily marked degree over the material." And he adds: "We believe that there is a spiritual nature in man responsive to the Divine Spirit, and that our spiritual nature can influence what we call our material nature. It often does so; in our own experience we have probably known cases where its influence has been very great. It is not, therefore, unreasonable to believe that spiritual nature can be so strengthened and inspired by God's Spirit as to make its power more effective."

Unless, then, we have given up belief in a personal God—that is, a God who has within Himself something corresponding to personal power in us—there is no reason for giving up the further belief that there are, behind nature, possibilities of a directive will similar in action to the directive energy within us, though infinitely more powerful and at present acting in mysterious hidden ways and apparently only at supremely critical times. In other words, we may say, with Bishop Gore, that "human personality, which is the highest form of life known to nature, is a better image of God than physical forces or chemical combinations. Call God, if you will, supernatural, but at any rate you must think of Him as not inferior to man. Here, then, we have a conception of God which is in no way antagonistic to the reign of law in nature, but which gives it a new meaning. The very nature of God is law and order. Nothing arbitrary or disconnected in action can be conceived of in connection with Him. But the principle of the order of nature is now seen to be, not blind mechanism, but the perfect reason and the perfectly free will of the supreme Creator."

There is no ground for the assumption that the physical world—the world of constant physical sequence and invariable law—is a self-completed and closed world, which can admit no influence from any other world. The evidence is against this theory of a self-complete enclosure; it cannot account for the action of human wills; it binds in chains a personal God, making Him less free than His creatures. There are many signs that scientists today are themselves in revolt against such a conception of the world.

[162]

We may be quite justified in laying as little stress as we consistently can on miracles, remembering that the great proof of the Christian faith is the person of its Founder; yet we should also bear in mind that many of his mighty works—those of healing, for example, as we have just seen—are becoming increasingly more credible in the light of modern psychology; and we may rightly look for new knowledge which will increase the credibility of others. If we regard the works of Christ as evidences of the extraordinary power of an extraordinary person, with extraordinary spiritual gifts and an extraordinary nature, we shall be on the right path toward a fuller understanding of mysteries that have always required faith for their explanation.

It is clear that some of the recorded miracles of Christ cannot, by any twist of the imagination, be accounted for as it is possible to explain the miracles of healing. But they are, to say the least, more credible as miracles than anything by way of explanation which has ever been substituted, or which men have tried to substitute for them. The miracles of the Gospels harmonize with the picture in which they have their setting. To use Headlam's words: "They are restrained; they are beneficent; they are not made the main purpose of the ministry; they take their place as something characteristic but subordinate; they ex-

[163]

hibit the same spiritual power as the words and work of Jesus."

In presenting the truth of Christianity, we must be on our guard lest we put the emphasis on miracles in such a way as to dislocate the order. We do not believe in Christ because of miracles; in spite of doubt and difficulty, we accept miracles because of Christ. His life and teaching were the gradual revelation of a divine person to other spiritually minded persons. His personality slowly impressed itself upon his followers until they came to see that it was unique, so unapproachable as to be explained only as a special intervention of God on behalf of men. His authority, his power, the dignity of his claims, the beauty of his character, the truth of his teaching, the wonder of his conception of God, the new view of life which he revealed, the perpetual experience of him which came to those who accepted him and his view of God and human life— these all joined to create the impression of him which has been incorporated in the faith of the ages. God being specially present, incarnate in human life, we look for miracles as of natural expectation under these conditions. That He was so present in the person of Christ, we may hope to see still more clearly before we close our study of his life.

Chapter XVI: A Doctor and His Clinic

NE aspect of the teaching of Christ
seems to have dropped out of consideration among the mass of Prot-
estant people today—his sacramental
teaching. In him was life. He declared that he
was the life of the world, the Bread of God which
came down from heaven. To the woman of
Samaria he said that with him was a well of water
springing into eternal life. He talked to Nicodemus in a mysterious way about this source of
new life. He spoke even more mysteriously in the
address which John records as having been given
in Capernaum after the feeding of the five thousand. The other evangelists do not record this
address, but this no more proves that it was
never given than does the fact that John fails
to record the institution of the Lord's Supper
prove that those who do tell about it were drawing too vividly upon their imagination. It is
plainly to be seen that John omits what the others
have recorded, and often, by way of teaching, in-
serts something bearing on the occasion which
they have omitted.

This sacramental element in Christ's doctrine

may fitly be introduced here in connection with his healing miracles. There is a noticeable feature —a peculiar method—in his work which may suggest an interesting line of thought.

The Good Physician had a company of pupils who watched him at his work. He was like a surgeon in a clinic, with the eyes of his students fixed upon him. Everywhere, the little company of his disciples went with him on his errands of mercy. As the tide of patients swept in upon him, the disciples noticed a strange thing about the Master's work of healing. They were slowly coming to believe that all power was given him, and yet he seemed to exercise that power only within limitations. They felt that he could heal by a word; yet with the crowds pressing him he chose a slower, plodding way.

What, then, was the remarkable thing that the twelve disciples learned as they watched the divine healer? This first: that instead of healing them all by a word, instead of willing cures by the wholesale, he took his patients one by one. And then, second—and we need to fix our attention upon this—that as each individual came to him for treatment, he almost always made use of material things in effecting his cures.

Remember that the apostles believed in his power to heal; believed that he might have healed all who came by the simple exercise of that power, without any assistance from without. What must have been their thoughts when they saw how he chose to work? Some material object seemed always to be the medium through which the healing was effected. Now it is the common clay; now the water of Siloam; now his own body; his hands; the saliva from his lips; even his garments. There was a man born deaf and with an impediment in his speech; Jesus took him aside from the multitude, put his fingers into the man's ears, touched his tongue. A blind man came to him; he spat on the ground, made clay of the spittle, anointed his eyes, and sent him to the pool to wash.

Out of all the recorded miracles of healing there are only five which were not accompanied by the use of some material object or physical agency, and in each of these cases there is a special reason for the variation from his customary method. Usually, ordinarily, he used material helps; and of the numerous other miraculous cures of which there is no detailed record, it is said that "he laid his hands upon them and healed them every one."

Now mark. He did this in spite of the apparent peril of arousing among the people a dangerous superstition. We know how easy it is for ignorant people to attribute a cure to some special object. Pilgrimages to the shrines of saints are not unknown today, and many cures have been attributed to the virtue of holy relics.

There was always that danger when Jesus the Good Physician wrought his cures: the danger that instead of attention being fixed upon himself alone, it might be fixed upon the things he used, and the cure attributed to some healing quality of the particular clay or water; it might be supposed that there was virtue in the touch of his garment; men's minds might be directed away from the healer; they might forget him and remember only the materials he employed.

Why, then, did he persist in his method? Must not the apostles have asked that question again and again? What did he mean? There they were, students in a clinic, watching the Master at his work, feeling that he wanted their attention, and that he had some purpose in arousing their questioning. Why did he do it that way?

We can think of but one answer. His purpose was to accustom the disciples to the use of material things in the conveying of physical gifts of healing, until at length they could grasp the thought that in the same way he meant to make use of material things in the conveying of spiritual gifts. In other words, he was preparing them for a great principle of the Christian religion, viz., the sacramental principle, that grace is conveyed to the soul "through channels." The things of earth are used to bring to men the gifts of heaven. Through things visible we are brought to an appreciation of things invisible.

So, as they question in their hearts, he speaks to them by and by of baptism; he tells Nicodemus that one must be born again of water and the Spirit; at the close of his ministry, he sends out his disciples to administer baptismal grace in the name of the Father, and of the Son, and of the Holy Spirit. Again, he tells them that their life must be fed from him; that except they eat the flesh of the Son of Man and drink his blood, they have no life in them; and long after, when there has been time for the thought to sink into their minds, he takes bread and wine, blesses it, and tells them that this is the body and blood of which he had spoken. When the day comes to send them forth as the Father had sent him, he lays his hands upon them and breathes on them, that in this very act their faith may be stimulated to believe in the fact of the in-flowing grace.

Why did Jesus Christ employ such a method? Perhaps because it is the simplest way to bring us to a realization of spiritual things. By Christ's sacramental method, faith is stimulated by sense. As in the miracles of healing the touch of the hand, the finger on the tongue, the clay on the eyes, the water of the pool, aroused the faith of those who were to be healed, made them ready and expectant, helped them to feel that something was being done for them—so now there is something we can see, touch, taste, handle, that faith may be quickened. The outward symbol is a pledge to assure us of grace given, as well as a means to its reception.

And not only an aid to faith, but a test of faith. It is enough that Christ has given the command; the faithful follower obeys, whether he understands or not. It is to be expected that one who submits loyally and obediently to a command or expressed wish of Christ will receive a blessing. "If a man opens his heart wide in loving response to the wish of another, that person's spirit inevitably enters. We see this sacramental act of receiving the spirit of another in every child who obeys, from a glad love, his father or his mother, in every student who tries hard to fulfill his great master's will for him, in every friend who from love tries to please his friend." Jesus Christ asks us to seek grace this way. It is a faith test —and we obey.

After all, we are souls in bodies. The body is the expression of the life of the soul. We shall always be souls in bodies; in the life of the world to come the soul will have that through which its life is expressed. Therefore the redemption of the soul will be the redemption of the body as well; and it is fitting that the gift to the soul should come through physical channels, so that every part of our nature may share in the bestowal of grace.

Chapter XVII: Going Up To Jerusalem

OW we are coming to the close of the Lord's ministry. When we interrupted the story, he and his companions were on their way going up to Jerusalem for the Passover. It was by no means the gay and joyous pilgrimage they had looked forward to, remembering other years when they had been a part of the happy-hearted crowds who always went singing on their way to the great festival.

It had begun to dawn on the apostles by this time that there lay before them no easy road to victory. There had been a time when all was fair and smiling, but now things were taking a different turn. The disciples were experiencing a rude awakening, and the way seemed ominously dark before them. Back in Galilee, even though of late the crowds had begun to drop away, their Master had for the most part found a ready hearing. On every side, at every village and town, people waited to receive him; they followed him into hill and country; they brought their sick to be healed; men and women blessed God as he drew near, and often his journeys became an enthusiastic, triumphal progress.

To be sure, the disciples had always alternated between expectation and disappointment. Always, just as he was at the point of acceptance and people were ready to hail him as a national hero, he had discouraged them by his teaching. To be sure, the Galilean folk were often as ready to drop a leader as they were to take him up. They were too eager to accept new ideas and to follow new popular idols, to make acceptance mean much. Being Galileans themselves, for the most part, the apostles knew this; but being Galileans they hardly faced the fact. What they saw was the present enthusiasm of the crowds who hailed their Master with delight, and they hoped for great things.

Then came the time when he began to warn them—twice already he had done so—about coming failure and death. They hardly understood, but they felt enough to dread this journey. They knew that at Jerusalem conservatism reigned. There, they knew, were the religious authorities and all the established order; there were the Roman power and the priestly caste, who, despite the superciliousness of the Pharisees, somehow seemed always bound strongly together when self-interest drew them.

And Jesus had aroused the antagonism, both of

the civil and of the religious rulers. It was plain that his reception in Jerusalem would not be friendly. Opposition was well under way and it would probably become harder and more bitter. The apostles began to see that if Jesus persisted in his purpose to go up for the feast, there was bound to be trouble, conflict, disaster. He himself had said that the journey would end in his death.

So, a few weeks before, Peter had presumed to remonstrate with Jesus about his plans: Why go to Jerusalem this year? Why not stay in Galilee awhile, win a larger following, strengthen our fellowship and bide our time until the outlook is more hopeful? The rebuke with which his Master met the suggestion shows how strong was the appeal; for that rebuke, so personal and so severe, would otherwise have been unwarranted.

Now they are again on the way. He had "set his face steadfastly to go up to Jerusalem." He knew that the storm was gathering, could hear its mutterings, felt that it was just ready to break; but he went on with determined purpose, not sadly nor despairingly, but sure, steady, strong, expectant, fearless. No wonder we read that "they were amazed and as they followed they were afraid." Yet they did follow, even though again he warned them of the impending issue. Thomas, always so blunt and matter-of-fact, but always loyal, expressed their loyalty also, when he said, as they went to Bethany, "Let us also go, that we may die with him."

On the way, they passed through Jericho. Here they met Zacchæus, whose penitent friendship the Master gained. Here they saw him restore sight to Bartimæus.

The blind man sat by the roadside begging. There are several accounts of the incident, and St. Matthew's Gospel says that there were two beggars. St. Mark's reads more like the report of an eyewitness. And Peter, whose memoirs Mark reports, was not likely, in his humbled mood, to forget anything that happened that day. One may easily picture the scene. The road was crowded with pilgrims. Among them, doubtless, were some of the "seventy other disciples" who had accepted Jesus. Some of "the women who followed him from Galilee" were there, and hundreds of others as well, together with the crowds who had come out from the city. What was the blind man thinking of, as he sat there hearing the crowd go by? How much did he know of the gossip of the road? Assuredly he had heard the people talking about Jesus, and possibly he had heard what some of these friends of his said. If the visit to Zacchæus had occurred the previous evening, he had probably heard the citizens discussing the action of this alleged Messiah in going to dine with a rich rogue. He remembered much that he had heard before of the prophet. Some called him only Jesus of Nazareth, and some spoke of him also as the Son of David, the Messiah.

Then something happened. The roar of the road struck a different note. There was a blockade of the people about him. He clutched one of the men in the crowd and asked what it was all about. They told him, "Jesus of Nazareth is passing by," and in a moment he made up his mind. Distinctly recognizing the Messianic claim and basing his petition on belief that Jesus had power and authority, he cried out, "Jesus, thou Son of David, have mercy on me." They tried to silence him; but he shouted all the louder, "O thou Son of David, have mercy on me." Then Jesus stopped and asked that the man be called. They told him of the summons and he, jumping up and throwing off his cloak, stumbled through the mob, helped by his friends, and came to Jesus. "Sir," he said, in answer to the question as to what he desired, "Sir, that I may receive my sight." "Go on your way," the Master replied, "your faith has made you well again," and at once his sight returned, and "he followed Jesus in the way."

The story is repeated here, because it is one

of many such reported miracles, illustrating the point already made, that no one but an eyewitness could have told the tale so vividly, that it bears about its recitation the marks of honest statement of fact, and that (believe what we may about miracles) it is difficult to read accounts such as these without feeling that their acceptance makes less of a demand on us than the attempt, by some curious perversion, to try to explain them away.

"And he followed Jesus in the way." One wonders what the man did, whom he met, how swiftly his faith grew, during the week that followed. Did he ever see Jesus again? Did he come to know any of the company more intimately? Was he at the crucifixion? Did he become one of the group of the faithful who afterward told of the resurrection triumph? Meanwhile, now that he was following with the others, did he impart fresh courage to them by his own faith and through their knowledge that the Master's power was still able to save? Or did they still move on in the terror of anticipation whose very uncertainty made them the more fearful?

As they moved toward Jerusalem, the twelve must have been turning over in their minds many things that had happened in the three years they had been with their Lord. These had been years of alternate hope and doubting uncertainty.

Of one thing, some of them had felt sure from the first: that their Master was the long-promised Messiah. This belief had grown in strength, despite the shocks of readjustment through which they came to a new understanding of what sort of Messiah he was to be. It was after Christ had deliberately led them away from any expectation of his taking his kingdom and reigning, after the fickle Galilean crowds had begun to melt away because of his refusal to do so, that Peter made his great declaration of faith, "Thou art the Messiah, the Son of the Living God."

What did they understand by the term "Son of God"? Probably very little, as yet. It was one of the titles of the Messiah and they were uncertain of its meaning. But they must have been absorbing significant ideas about the name, even though (quite naturally) they had not yet tried to formulate these ideas.

Son of Man? My Beloved Son? The Holy One of God? Peter remembered an occasion when he had thoughtlessly pledged his Master's word for the payment of the "temple tax," a special assessment levied in the month Adar for the maintenance of the regular worship at Jerusalem. Jesus had said a strange thing that day. "Of whom do the kings of the earth exact taxes," he asked, "of their own sons, or of the sons of others?" And when Peter gave the natural answer, Jesus said, "Then would not the King's sons be free?" What did he mean? The words were capable of weighty import, inasmuch as the tax was for the support of the temple worship of the King of Kings. Or they might be a mere bantering bit of pleasantry—for, apparently, the story which follows of the coin found in the mouth of a fish is not the record of a miracle; it is not said that Peter actually went fishing to find the coin; only, perhaps, that he was smilingly bidden to do so.

Son? Did that account for the glory of his face on the Mount of Transfiguration? And what were the mysterious voices they heard that day? Put yourself in their place, not having any clearer ideas than they then had of Christ's real nature, and you would hardly know what you had seen or heard; certainly you would not know what you had thought or ought to think. That is the way Peter felt; he could only stumble through a few words about building a shrine there for Jesus.

Son? Was that why he spoke with such authority? Did that explain why, when he was with them, God seemed so near? And did it help them to understand, when he spoke, why God seemed so real? Who was this man who so quietly revised the God-given law of Moses with a note of calm authority; who laid down conditions upon which one might enter the Kingdom of Heaven; who boldly said that he came to fulfill the law, not to destroy it, as if there could be any question as to its destruction; who made claims unlike anything a prophet had ever made before; who actually declared what sort of sin was unforgivable and what standard of righteousness acceptable?

And then his claim to forgive sins—what did that mean? There was no question as to what the Pharisees thought about it when he uttered absolving words before healing the young paralytic in Capernaum; they accused him of blasphemy in usurping a divine prerogative, and his only answer had been an act of healing by which he demonstrated his right to forgive.

Son of God? One can see that they would not take in all the meaning, even although they had long before this heard him say, "No man knows the Son but the Father, nor does anyone know the Father but the Son, and he to whom the Son will reveal him."

It should always be remembered (apart from the question of what the apostles actually did believe about Jesus) that they came to whatever their faith was very slowly, with many stumblings toward the truth and many uncertainties, and even after the resurrection with much dimness of perception.

Now, however, on the road to Jerusalem, as he pressed forward eagerly and they followed timidly, they must have done much thinking. What did they think about his mighty works? Had they ever asked whether the most wonderful Messiah ever dreamed of could do these things? They believed he had wrought great deeds, even that he had raised the dead, however hard it may be for some to believe it today—what did they think about it all? What did they believe? They hardly knew—they felt more than they could even begin to express. One thing was apparent: they were practically treating him as they would treat God, acting toward him as toward God, relying on him as on no human friend and helper. Only: not yet had they asked why.

What did it mean? They did not know. All that they knew was that they loved him. And now they were afraid—afraid for him as well as for themselves.

The Pharisees hated him, because he had broken their Sabbath rules, had been careless of ceremonials which they considered inspired rites, had denounced them for the cold-heartedness of their religion, a religion that made them careful of tithing, but careless of acts of oppression toward the poor; hated him, because many a time he had declared that even the lowest of the people, the scum of society, had better chances of heaven than their own. They hated him for the "woes" he pronounced against them, for the parables he evidently intended should be applied to them, for the attack upon their practices, even as the Sadducees hated him for imperiling their perquisites.

Others honestly doubted. They sincerely believed that he was a dangerous radical. Some naturally opposed him as a blasphemer who made himself like unto God and deserved death for his sin as well as because of his dangerous doctrine.

And the apostles: They could only go stumbling on, remembering that he had said, "If you are ashamed of me and of my words, then will I also be ashamed of you, when I come again, in the glory of the Father, and with the holy angels." They could only follow, like Thomas, even though they marched to death; because he had said, "If anyone would come after me, let him take up his cross and follow." They never dreamed that they could be anything but faithful to the end; because he had said, "What profit is it to a man, if he gain the whole world and yet forfeit his soul?"

So they went on from Jericho to Jerusalem; and six days before the Passover, he rested in Bethany before going into the city with his troubled friends.

Chapter XVIII: The Days of Lost Opportunity

HE restful night in Bethany must have driven away the fears that had haunted the apostles for days. They seem to have awakened to a happy morning; and when their Master announced his preparations for entrance into the city, they set about in bright anticipation of a joyous festival.

It is not easy to determine exactly the meaning of the Palm Sunday entrance. Some have supposed that Jesus, this once, in the effort to give the nation one more chance, allowed himself to meet the expectation of the people and to bend to their wishes. If so, he had in mind an ancient writing, which told how the Messiah should come to Israel—a king, riding on a royal beast; but not a warrior king, a man of peace. For this reason, he sent two of his friends into the neighboring village of Bethphage and told them to bring the ass and the colt they would find tethered at the entrance to the village. Warrior kings rode on horses; when kings went on peaceful errands, they went on asses.

All this seems a little stilted, an approach to the dramatic quite unlike Christ. It is much more probable that he made the preparations for his entrance into Jerusalem in a quiet way, though preferring not to go quite so simply as on his teaching journeys. The crowds that greeted him made the entrance more of a spectacle than was his intention, and afterward his disciples remembered that one of the old prophets had written about the coming of the King in words that were singularly appropriate to the events of this day.

So Jesus and his followers began the journey to Jerusalem. The Twelve forgot their fears in their rejoicing over the welcome he received. The news of the raising of Lazarus had spread, and on all hands people were asking whether the wonderworker who had done this thing would come to the feast. The religious leaders also wondered, but for a very different reason. They had come to the conclusion that he was a dangerous man. To all their other reasons for hating him, there was added now the fear that if he rode long on this wave of popularity the people would sweep him into rebellion against Rome and to an assertion of national independence. That, of course, could end only in failure, and then they would lose their place and nation. Very subtly the High Priest, who had reasons of his own for hating Jesus, argued that it was best that one man should die for the people and not that the whole nation perish—unconscious, of course, of the meaning later to be placed on his words. "Indeed, yes," said one of the apostles afterward; "not for this nation only, but to gather together into one all God's dispersed children." Caiaphas spoke better than he knew when he said that Jesus should die for the people; his official position as High Priest gave his words prophetic meaning.

So the priests plotted, while the people rejoiced. On Jesus moved toward Jerusalem, up the road, around the brow of the hill. Other pilgrims joined the company. Still others, anxious to see the Galilean prophet, came out from Jerusalem to meet the party, as, indeed, they often met other companies coming up from various parts of the country. Meeting him, they waved their palm branches. Soon some enthusiasts began to throw down these branches to make a carpet on which the prophet might ride; others tore off branches from the trees and cast them before him; this soon became general, after the custom of those who would welcome a king. Then some took off their cloaks and spread them in the road. Meanwhile, unconscious of its deeper significance, they sang their psalm, "Hosanna to the Son of David! Blessed is He that cometh in the Name of the Lord. Hosanna in the highest!"—unconscious also of its fulfilment of one of the words of Jesus himself, who had evidently believed that he would have his moment of partial recognition before the tragic end of his career—or was it that afterward, that week, in his attack on the Pharisees, he reminded them of the meaning which they had not discerned?

So they moved on. The disciples felt that at last his cause was laying hold on the nation. They forgot their former misgivings. They were sure that great and glorious events would follow this glorious day. They hardly knew what they expected, but at any rate they felt that it would be a mighty triumph for him. After all, his trip into "the enemy's country" was not turning out badly! With happy hearts, they joined the singing crowd. They were full of anticipations of the coming glory.

Then a sudden hush. The gladness went out of their faces, the joy was stilled in their hearts, they looked at each other in amazement: the Master was crying! Evidently he had no illusions; he knew that this wave of excitement would soon pass. They had just turned the brow of the hill and before them lay Jerusalem with its turrets and towers; and he burst into tears at the sight. He saw the city and he saw its future fate; its eager crowd of pilgrims and their real spiritual state. This which was their day of opportunity was passing and its coming had been in vain.

"If thou hadst known, even thou, at least in this thy day, the things which belong unto thy peace! But now they are hid from thine eyes. For the days shall come unto thee, that thine enemies shall cast a trench about thee, and compass thee round, and keep thee in on every side, and shall lay thee even with the ground, and thy children within thee; and they shall not leave in thee one stone upon another; because thou knewest not the time of thy visitation."

Later in the same week he uttered words of similar tender grief; the more remarkable in that they came at the end of his stern denunciation of the Pharisees and therefore show how even in rebuke he was still full of love and longing for them: "O Jerusalem, Jerusalem, thou that killest the prophets, and stonest them that are sent unto thee, how often would I have gathered thy children together, even as a hen gathereth her chickens under her wings, and ye would not! Behold, your house is left unto you desolate."

We must hurry on. Probably the attack upon the traffickers in the temple followed the Palm Sunday triumph. St. John, who is supposed to have written for the purpose of correcting some errors (especially of chronology) in the other Gospels, does not mention it here, but has told of a similar scene in the beginning of the ministry.

There seems to be no reason why the action with which Jesus began his ministry should not have been repeated at its close, when he saw again how small had been the effect of his former indignant attack. And it would account, also, for the increasing fury of the Pharisees, as well as for their demand that he should tell them by what authority he was exercising his powers as a reformer.

Possibly, however, he remained in the temple only long enough to worship; long enough, however, to notice the poor widow's gift at the treasury, and long enough to be greeted in joyous acclaim by the children. "Out of the mouths of babes and sucklings thou didst perfect praise."

During the week there are various encounters with the rulers; he taught in parables to the people; answered the insidious questions of the Pharisees, who tried to trap him with an inquiry about the tribute money; of the Sadducees, who asked him some frivolous questions about marriage in the resurrection age; of a lawyer, who wanted to know about the first and great commandment. Later there came the terrible indictment of the Pharisees which Matthew reports in full.

One curious and unforgettable circumstance is related among the events of the week. There were Gentile proselytes who had been so far won to the faith of Israel that they worshipped in the temple and went up to Jerusalem for the great festivals. Among them on this occasion were some Greeks who desired to see Jesus. They applied first to Philip, who came from a city where there were many Greek inhabitants, and Philip in turn took them to Andrew. The two introduced them to the Master. The visit seems to have brought to him a renewal of the old temptation. Now as he feels death advancing, he asks again, Why must it be? Perhaps he saw in vision the possibilities of acceptance outside his own people; perhaps it was dread of impending fate. At any rate he prayed, prayed in words that were spoken brokenly in the very midst of a reply to his visitors. In reading the account, it is not easy to see where speech with the Greeks ends and speech with God begins.

First he spoke to the visitors: "The hour is come that the Son of Man should be glorified. Truly I say to you, only as the kernel of the wheat falls into the ground, there to die, can it bear fruit; if it does not die, it lies there alone. So one who loves his life really loses life, and he who hates life as it is bound up with this world shall keep it unto life eternal. If any man would serve me, let him follow me, and where I am there also shall my servant be. If any man (that is, Jew or Gentile) serve me, him will my Father honor."

Then: "Now is my soul troubled. And what shall I say—Father, save me from this hour? But for this cause I came to this hour. Father, glorify thy name."

Then a voice from heaven, bringing him assurance—a voice which he heard and which some who stood by thought they heard also, but which others said was only distant rolling thunder. And then one sentence more, showing he knew that the hour of death was near, but showing also his assurance that his death was to be the life of men, and giving evidence that his sacrifice would be for all the world, Jew and Gentile:

"Now is the judgment of this world. Now shall the prince of this world be cast out. And I, if I be lifted up, will draw all men unto me."

That night—Wednesday of his last week— he spent in prayer on the Mount of Olives; as, so we are told, he spent every night except the night of the Supper. All of Thursday was spent in quiet, apparently, gathering strength for the final trial. He was following advice he had more than once given his disciples, "Come ye yourselves apart, and rest awhile."

Chapter XIX: Jesus at Prayer

IT MAY not be out of place to interrupt the narrative at this point to consider Jesus at prayer. Prayer seems always to have been his source of strength in meeting the duties and work of life. During this last week, so full of work and care, full of temptation and of anxiety lest his followers fail when he himself had carried through his great work, we read of long periods of communion with God his Father. "In the daytime he was teaching in the temple; at night he went out, and abode in the mount that is called the Mount of Olives," in quiet devotion.

All his life long he lived in spiritual communion. Prayer was the breath of his life. We read of occasions when he "spent the whole night in prayer," of others when "he rose a great while before it was day," or "while it was yet dark" to begin the day in converse with the Father. He spent such a night in prayer before he chose the twelve apostles; and again before he asked the momentous question of Peter, "Who do you say that I am?" He prayed in an agony of supplication in the garden of Gethsemane. On the cross he prayed for his executioners. Dying there as a criminal, suffering intense physical pain, deserted by friends and surrounded by taunting enemies, he died in deepest and fullest communion with God, breathing a prayer to the Father of whose love he was always certain and in whose presence he felt safe.

It makes plain his complete humanity. The men who had faithfully followed him soon came to proclaim their unfailing faith that in "all the time that the Lord Jesus went in and out among them" they had been walking and talking with God—so that their eyes had actually gazed upon and their hands had handled the Word of Life. Yet they never lost faith that, although he was God, he had become completely human, manifesting the life of God in human nature and living with human strength, meeting temptation with human weapons.

Why did he pray? Because in coming among men he had laid aside his divine majesty and had come to live a man's life under its ordinary conditions and with such powers and faculties as other men have. He prayed, therefore, because prayer is the source of strength for human kind. It was needful for him, as for others, to be "in tune with the infinite"; he must preserve fellowship with the Father if he would know the Father's will and be strong to do it.

[192]

There was very little of petition in the prayers of Christ. He rarely asked anything for himself, though occasionally he did make such requests. His prayers were such as took him into his Father's presence for something more than petition—for worship. "Show thou me the way that I should walk in, for I lift up my soul unto thee."

There was very little of self in his prayers. The great prayer which he taught his disciples is all in the plural:

Our Father, who art in heaven, hallowed be thy name, thy kingdom come, thy will be done, as in heaven, so also upon the earth. Give us daily our food for the approaching day. Forgive us our debts, as we also have forgiven our debtors. And lead us not into temptation, but rescue us from the Evil One.

The prayer, Luke tells us, was given the disciples on an occasion when they came upon him at his devotions. Seeing him, they realized what prayer could be, and asked him to teach them how to pray. They wanted, too, some form of prayer, as John had given a form to his followers. The prayer that Jesus gave them was a model, rather than a formal or set prayer; yet he repeated it, possibly, on other occasions and is said to have made it a part of his address on the

Mount. It may rightly, therefore, be used as a form, provided the form be filled with the spirit of devotion. The prayer is simple, brief, spiritual, clear in meaning, save for some difficulty as to the last petition. The point made here, however, is that there is so little of self in it. It is all in the plural. One cannot use it for one's self alone. Once more: this prayer is spiritual, full of God, the longing for his glory, the coming of his kingdom, the fulfillment of His purpose; full of the desire to keep His name sacred. All of Christ's recorded prayers were of the same spirit.

He prayed, so far as he himself was concerned, for direction, guidance and strength. The purpose of prayer is not to bend God's will to our own will, but to bring our wills into submission to the divine purpose. In Gethsemane, Christ uttered a prayer which seemed not to have been answered; the answer really came in the gradual disclosure of the Father's will.

One sees it as the prayer continues: First: *"If it be possible,* let this cup pass from me"; then, *"If this cup may not pass* from me except I drink it, thy will be done"; three times, "Nevertheless, not as I will, but as thou wilt." Then "there appeared an angel from heaven strengthening him." It was prayer which made God's will clear and gave strength to submit to it.

The same note is found in the most beautiful

[194]

of all prayers, the great sacerdotal intercession uttered on the night of the Last Supper and recorded in the seventeenth chapter of St. John's Gospel. Here also prayer is found to be unselfish; if he asks that the Son be glorified, it is only that so the disciples may see, believe, and be kept faithful.

What about prayer for ourselves? We remember our own prayers as children, when we asked God for anything and everything: good weather for a holiday, the gifts we wanted at Christmas, all the simple desires of childish hearts. We had the childlike spirit which Christ asked of his disciples, because we had not yet grown out of childhood days.

Then one day we waked up—waked to the disappointment of unanswered desire. After that, the blows came thick and fast. In time of danger we prayed, but the danger did not pass; in time of impending sorrow, but death came none the less certainly; in time of mental or spiritual distress, but the heavens were closed and God did not answer. We began to understand that God rules by laws which He cannot or will not break; that there are laws of health, and they work with inevitable regularity; laws of economics, and financial ruin follows their violation; laws of nature, and though slow of operation they are always sure. We gave up. Prayer could not do what we had, in childhood days, believed that it could do.

How, then, can we continue to pray, and what can we make of prayer, if we do continue? The answer is simple for one who believes in Jesus Christ as God, or, for the matter of that, even for one who thinks of him as the best man that ever lived. Whatever one may believe about him, his conception of God is richer than any other man has ever known. Why not try it out? The Christian believer goes further. He believes that Christ came from the bosom of the Father. He believes that Christ knew. He prays because Christ prayed. It is a right instinct that drives us to God. We take it on the word of Jesus himself, who "taught us to pray."

Our prayers, if we do pray, teach us something. The common conception of prayer is that it is an effort to bend God's purpose to our wish; and the sadness of the awakening is due to the discovery that the facts do not warrant the as·sumption. Thinking more of God, we find that He does rule the world by law and that to grant our prayer sometimes would, it is true, be to break a link in the chain of cause and effect and throw the universe into ungoverned disorder. What then? Does it mean that a great range

of petitions has become unlawful? Of course not.
As there are laws of nature and laws of health, so
there are spiritual laws, and our prayer may set
in motion forces that will counterbalance other
forces, just as by mechanics we can overcome the
law of gravitation. What do we know of the
spiritual world? May not God have laid down
its laws so that much of His giving shall be dependent upon our asking, exactly as the rich treasures of the earth—the grain in the fields, the
fruit on the trees, the wealth of the mines—are
all of them ours only when we have done our
part to earn them?

Shall we give up prayer in sickness, for example? The laws of psychotherapy are beginning to show us that more things are done by
prayer than this world dreams of. Perhaps, after
all, our faith has never been very great, and our
prayers for a sick friend have been offered with
no decided belief or expectation. "All things that
you ask, believing," was the way Christ put it;
and we have been praying always with the thought
in the background that the prayer could not avail.
Of course it may not. In the face of facts—
bitter facts of experience for others as well as for
ourselves—we know that there are laws which
no prayer will ever overcome. But we pray on,
nevertheless, and when the answer does not come,
sometimes at least we see more clearly.

One thing we see is that God often answers prayer through human agents and in human work. The skill and understanding of the physician; the new health laws which medical science is constantly discovering; above all, the deeper sympathy with the world's pain and the quickened desire to help which have lightened to such an extent the world's burden—who knows what part prayer has had in all this? The spirit of social service which has brought light into so many dark places and made human life so much less hard to endure—who can say how much prayer had to do with the enlightenment? The new sense of corporate responsibility, with its education toward a better industrial order—has prayer had nothing to do with opening our eyes there? There is indeed an "intercession which is co-operation with God"; and God has been showing us many things of late of which the world has long been ignorant. The growth of the social spirit as a late fruit of Christianity may "make possible the rebirth of a Christian community which can become the strongest force in the world." Prayer pointed out the path of progress.

So we pray because Jesus Christ prayed; and we try to pray as he prayed. "The Son of Man feels the hour at hand; shrinks from it, flies from human society—feels the need of it again, and goes back to his disciples. Here is that need of sympathy which forces us to seek for it among relatives and friends; and here is that recoil which forces us back to our loneliness again. In such an hour they who have before forgotten prayer betake themselves to God, knowing that only with Him can perfect understanding and sympathy be found."

Chapter XX: Supper and Sacrament

I T is natural to pass from the Master's prayers to his Last Supper, for this was the occasion of his instituting the service which has been the great Christian act of remembrance of him during all the centuries since that evening when he sat with his disciples to eat with them the paschal feast, to speak with them in tenderest words of instruction, counsel, and farewell, and then to go forth to his passion and death.

The difficulty of harmonizing the accounts of the Gospel according to St. John with the accounts in the other Gospels makes it uncertain whether the supper at which the thirteen gathered was actually the ceremonial meal of the Passover night or a paschal supper arranged by anticipation for the previous evening. At any rate, it was held on Thursday night—ever since called Maundy Thursday, because it was the occasion of the giving of the New Commandment.

The room of meeting was possibly in the house of the parents of Mark the Evangelist. We are not sure. The unknown disciple who put at Christ's disposal this room where he might eat the Passover, in quietness and security, did the one thoughtful act which must have been most pleasing to his Master; but, like those of many another obscure disciple, his name and rank have never been known. The preparations had already been made, when in the late afternoon Jesus and the Twelve entered the city. After worshipping at the temple, they moved on to the house where the supper had been prepared.

Most of us know the story so well that it is hardly necessary to enter into details. It cannot fail to strike the imagination, in trying to picture the scene, to remember that for more than thirty-four centuries this night has never been forgotten as it comes each year. For fifteen hundred years the feast had been kept by faithful Jews as a memorial of their deliverance from the bondage of Egypt. For nineteen hundred years more it has been kept, in sacramental fulfilment of its promise, as a memorial of one who came, according to his own declaration, to deliver mankind from the bondage of sin.

Hardly had the guests reclined at the table, when a dispute arose among some of them as to which should have the seat of honor. Jesus said nothing. The supper proceeded. The cup of wine was mixed (which Jesus said he would "drink with them new in the kingdom") and then the various viands were passed about—the bitter herbs, symbolizing the bitterness of the Egyptian bondage, the unleavened bread, the roasted lamb. After the blessing had been given, the herbs and unleavened bread were dipped in the wine and eaten, and then came the second cup of blessing.

It was at this point that the youngest person present was, by custom, to ask of the Master of the feast the meaning of "this service." Just here, probably, Jesus arose, quietly stripped off his upper garments, tied a towel about his waist and taking a basin of water knelt to wash the feet of the disciples. He came to Peter first, apparently. One sees the astonishment and horror in the disciple's face. "Would you wash my feet?" "What I am doing you do not understand now; later you will know," said the Master. "No— never; never must you wash my feet." Jesus replied quietly that unless his feet were washed, he could have "no part with him," and then the disciple impulsively urged, "Not my feet only, then, but my hands and head." The answer that one who had bathed needed not to wash again, except to cleanse his feet, is probably a reference to the temple ritual, according to which the priests bathed before beginning the sacrificial service and then at stated intervals washed their feet of dust before beginning a new part of the ritual. Afterward the words came to symbolize the bath of regeneration in baptism, which is never repeated, though "the dust of sin" must daily be washed away.

"You are all clean," Jesus said, "but not all." Then, from man to man he went, kneeling and washing their feet, and then, reclining again at table, taught the lesson of humility of which their dispute over the place of honor clearly showed the need. I, your Lord and Master, have washed your feet, coming among you as one who does the work of a slave. I have given you an example of humble service. Be like-minded. Do as I have done.

At least twice, before they came up to Jerusalem, he had warned them of his approaching betrayal. Now he warned them again, with greater emphasis, for he brought home the fact that among themselves there was a traitor. He knew (for "he knew what was in a man") of the visit Judas of Kerioth had made to the priests that day, and now he said, "One of you shall betray me."

They were horrified; yet knowing their own weakness, they were also stricken in conscience, and one after another they asked in shuddering whispers, "Master, is it I?" "Is it I?" John had the place at the table next to Jesus, and to him Peter motioned that he should ask who it was that could do such a deed. The question was asked, and the reply given quietly, "He to whom I give the sop when I have dipped it"; and then, handing the sop to Judas, he said, "What you are about to do, do at once." And Judas went out into the night to seek again the priestly leaders and to plan for his Master's capture.

The man is a mystery. Why was he chosen? Was he Christ's one mistake? Or, if it cannot be imagined that he who so clearly read human nature could have made such a mistake, what was his purpose in choosing Judas? Was it that, near Jesus, he might have every possible chance? And what about the clash of human freedom and divine foreknowledge? It was once a subject which delighted the theological mind. Probably in this day most of us have come to the common-sense conclusion that such questions are among the insoluble mysteries and that we waste precious time in disputes about them—time that might be put to better use in brotherly service.

We cannot solve the mystery of Judas, as it has to do with his original choice; but we can see plainly how his downfall came about. That is, indeed, a useful subject of inquiry, because the tendency in other days was to set Judas by himself as the chief of sinners and to fail to see in him any likeness to one's self.

All the disciples had given their allegiance to

their Master without clear understanding of his purpose. All of them hoped that he would be accepted by the nation and take up his kingly office. The others gradually passed through a purifying process, as they lived with their Master and grew in love and loyalty. They had spiritual stuff in them that made them appreciate him even before they fully understood him. It was not so with Judas. When he discovered that there was to be no earthly kingdom, with material rewards or place and power for himself, he began to feel cheated, grew resentful, gradually came to the point where he felt that it would be best for him to get out before the crash came; and because he felt that he had been tricked and deceived, made up his mind to get all that he could out of the wreck before he left. He began, one account says, to steal from the common purse; he ended by becoming an informer for pay. When the tragedy was over, he was seized with remorse and committed suicide. He "went to his own place," and only the Infinite Mind knows whether or not remorse was touched with penitence at the last and whether his "place" was other than the abode to which he has been so readily consigned when his fate has been determined by men who ought to know in their own hearts the power of sin.

Jesus had foreseen it long before, and on the occasion of Peter's great declaration of faith had spoken words of warning that might have set the man's conscience working again; but every effort failed, and now he had done his black deed and was out in the night. But is he so different from others since? Are there not cool, hardhearted men today just as impatient of idealism as was Judas when he felt that his Master was foolishly persisting in an impossible course?

It is interesting to contrast him with Peter. Just at this break in the feast, the latter had boasted that even though others should find in their Master occasion of stumbling and so fall, he would never desert him. He was ready to go to prison and death. A few hours later he was sobbing out his heart, because he had failed tragically. The warning words of Christ which told how he would make denial three times before the morning's cock-crowing came back to his memory as "the cock crowed the second time."

After this followed the beautiful words of comfort and counsel which St. John alone reports. It has already been noted that recent historical criticism declares that the chapters which make up this record (St. John, Chapters XIV—XVII) seem to offer indubitable evidence of being the actual expression of the mind of Christ. It is difficult to see how one can deny it.

"Believe in God. Believe also in me. In my

Father's house are many mansions; surely I would have told you, were it not so. I go to prepare a place for you. If I go to prepare a place for you, I will come again to receive you to myself."

"I am the way, the truth, the life. No man comes to the Father, but through me."

"Have you been with me so long, and yet have you not known me? He who has seen me has seen the Father."

"If a man love me, he will keep my words, and my Father will love him, and we will come unto him and sojourn with him."

"I am the vine, you are all branches. Abide in me, even as I abide in you."

"If you keep my commandments, you will abide in my love, even as I have kept my Father's commandments and abide in his love."

"Love one another, as I have loved you. Greater love has no man than this, that a man lay down his life for his friends. You are my friends."

Immediately after this address, probably, came the institution of the new sacrament of love, the Holy Communion. Then came the great prayer, and then they went forth singing one of the psalms of the evening. Jesus led the eleven along the silent street, through the gate, and across the

Kedron, to a garden where he was accustomed to retire for devotion.

Here came the hours of prayer and agony already mentioned; here the tired apostles failed him in his hour of need; here the temple officials came to seize him; here there was a final lesson to Peter in the healing of the soldier at whose ear the impulsive apostle had cut wildly with his sword; here the traitor betrayed him with a kiss; here his manhood flashed out once more, in power, as he came out to meet his captors and they quailed before him and stumbled back, falling over one another in confusion.

Before we pass on to the trial and death, it will be well to go back to the supper; for the new rite which Jesus instituted then has now been the great service of Christian worship for nineteen centuries.

Chapter XXI: The Lord's Own Service

OR nineteen centuries, Christ has been remembered in the new feast which he instituted at the Passover Supper that night in the upper room. During all these centuries quiet groups have knelt in silent churches, with bowed heads, offering to him the acceptance and faith which his own generation denied. Let us go back again, then, to the scene of the institution.

Stop a moment and think. Your mother is dying. You sit by her bedside, her hand in yours. She looks up into your face. There are many things you both want to say; but you can neither of you bear them now. At length she does speak, in low, trembling tones, of things which must be said. She tells you what she wants you to do for her in the few days that are left. And then, with a smile that lights up her face, she speaks of some other thing she wants done afterward. "You will do it, dear," she asks, "do it for me? And you won't forget me, will you? Do it always, to remember me." What kind of a son would you be if you forgot?

The Lord Jesus Christ, who was the world's

friend, gathered his followers about him on the night before he died. He was divine; but he was very human. And he had all this human longing not to be forgotten; purged, of course, of all self-seeking—he would be remembered, not for his sake only, but for ours. He and his friends had met for a solemn and sacred purpose. They had kept together the Passover Supper, the great religious feast of their race. When it was over, he took bread and wine—the paschal bread of the feast and the wine mingled with water. He raised his hands in blessing; he broke the bread and poured out the wine; he told them that his own body would be broken and his blood shed for them. And then he said: Do this always in remembrance of me.

What kind of Christians are we if we forget?

So we think of the Holy Communion first as a devout act of remembrance. If one cannot believe any more than that about it, yet it is possible to come acceptably. But it is more than that. In some way it has always been felt that in this service Jesus Christ touches us, and we receive his very life.

Let us think a moment about ourselves. You cannot see me; I cannot see you. All that you see of me—this hand; this face—is not myself; it is the garment my spirit wears. What you see is only carbon, phosphorus, lime and water and a little sodium chloride mixed. But God breathed upon this material body and it became a living soul. That soul is my real self, though you cannot see it.

The mother's kiss: it is only a little dust of her lips touching the dust of your forehead. Is it? Or is it the fellowship of her spirit with yours in the power of love? The mother's tears: they are only a little water and a pinch of salt. Or are they more?

And Jesus Christ said wonderful things about this sacrament of his love. He said: "This is my body; this is my blood."

It will be objected that he was speaking figuratively. Of course he was. But what do we mean by figurative language, unless it be that our figures of speech are an effort to express a bigger truth than we can put into humdrum prose? The very need of figurative language shows that the idea to which we are trying to give utterance calls for a heavier burden of meaning than ordinary words can bear. To say that words are figurative is not to empty them of meaning. It is to say that the wider conception must be at least as great as the figure itself.

Let us be frank to declare, therefore, that these words of Christ are figurative. What then? Why, this: that the inner reality which needs such a figure to express it must be great beyond all thought. We are not making the Holy Communion less mysterious, then, if we call the language that describes it a figurative language; we have but deepened the mystery.

That is the next thing we must feel, then, about the Holy Communion. It is not merely an act of remembrance; it is Christ's way of giving us his life. He himself is present when we do what he commanded. The food we take is not material food only; it is his very life. "The cup of blessing which we bless, is it not the communion of the Blood of Christ? The bread which we break, is it not the communion of the Body of Christ?" So St. Paul puts the question and those who accept our Lord's words on their face value can give but an affirmative answer.

When our Lord said, "Do this in remembrance of me," what he chose to be remembered for is significant. He was famous for his teaching, and yet more notable for his wondrous works. Yet he chose neither. He would be remembered in his death. That was because his death was no ordinary martyrdom. He gave his life a ransom for many. His death was a propitiatory sacrifice for the sin of the world. Into the world of sin, divine forgiveness came freely; but it came by divine love itself bearing, before our eyes, our sins or their results. In the death of Christ, as in nothing else, we see the awfulness of sin, and are brought to acknowledge the penalty that is its due. There, as nowhere else, the pain and the shame of sin are awakened. In the supreme moment of forgiveness, we find that forgiveness is made possible because at last we have seen sin with the eyes of God.

It was this that the Lord would bring constantly to our remembrance; and so he said, "Do this." The words probably have a meaning deeper than our first thought would suggest. They are sacrificial words; perhaps they would best be translated, "Offer this for my memorial." And so the Holy Communion is not simply an act of remembrance, nor is it only the means of approach to the divine presence; it is a sacrificial service.

Not until men have grown into fuller appreciation of "the Lord's own service" shall we ever know what public worship is, and so it has not seemed out of place to dwell at length on the original institution. Those who wrote the Gospels linger lovingly over the details. The story of the last night occupies much of their space, because it held so large a place in their hearts.

Chapter XXII: The Tragic Ending

OUBTLESS some who have read thus far these simple studies in the life of Jesus Christ have felt a lack of proportion in the treatment. Only toward the close of his life have we given the story in much detail. But is not that the Gospel method? There are fifteen chapters in St. Mark's Gospel, and five of them—and these the longest—are devoted to the story of Christ's last week. St. Matthew usually condenses the material used in St. Mark—and often with a loss of the vividness and warmth of the original—in order that he may present in fuller form the Lord's teaching; yet he gives seven long chapters to this last week. St. Luke is no briefer. St. John gives eight chapters out of twenty-one. The early evangelists looked upon the passion and death of Christ as something of such tremendous import that they lingered over the story as over no other part of his life.

Why? Probably, to a certain extent, because they felt so keenly their own failure. It is characteristic of the evangelistic narratives that they never spared the apostles. That is one reason for accepting these narratives as authentic. Now and then, in the later Gospel, there are evidences of a willingness to alter earlier phraseology in order to correct a possible misapprehension about Jesus himself. This is one of the characteristics of the Gospels that clearly disproves the theory of the verbal inspiration and literal inerrancy of Holy Scripture. But however jealous the writers may be to guard against misunderstandings about their Master, they have nothing to conceal or explain about themselves. They had been bowed to the dust at the recollection of their cowardice, and they wanted their deeds known, that their penitence might be attested and their restoration appreciated. They did not hide their own stupidities, blunders, or weaknesses in any part of the story; and because their sin in those days when they forsook him and fled seemed so awful in retrospect, they told more of this week than of the whole three years of the Lord's life. What they told has been as faithfully cherished by the Gospel "editors" and as fully recorded.

That does not explain all, however. They told more of this week, because this week, its tragic sacrifice and its subsequent glorious victory, meant more. Looking back, they saw how much it meant to Jesus himself, how often he had warned them of the approaching death and of the rising on the third day—though this last seems to have passed through their minds without conscious impression, in their agitation over the prophecy of the failure and the apparently futile ending of his career. Looking back, they remembered these premonitions of the approaching tragedy. Looking back, they remembered, too, that it overwhelmed them and left them appalled when the blow fell, despite these warnings. Looking back, they remembered the words with which he soothed their anxious hearts that week, and they wished to put down every sentence. Looking back from the glorious Easter victory, they saw the tremendous significance of his cross and passion, and so they told the story with fascinated interest as well as penitent shame.

After all, was there ever a death like this? Who else ever spoke as Jesus spoke of giving his life "a ransom for many"? Who else ever prophesied the manner of his death, and said that through his sacrifice he would "draw all men unto himself"? Who else ever emphasized the purpose of his life as an effort "to seek and to save those that are lost"? Who else ever chose his death as that by which he would be remembered, or spoke of his body and blood as the food of spiritual life?

If we accept St. John's Gospel as a substantially accurate interpretation of the teaching of Christ, we find the struggle taking on the semblance of a deliberately offered sacrifice, with solemn words of priestly intercession and the surrender of himself as a victim for the sin of the world. "Greater love has no man than this, that a man lay down his life for his friends."

And an accurate record it seems to be. We may say that we do not understand it, or feel that it appears to be an overdrawn or metaphysical interpretation; but it is difficult to see how one can read it with indifference, or read it without feeling (whether he understands or not) that as he reads he has come nearer than anywhere else to the presence of Christ. Then, too, when this truth has come home to us, we see broken lights of a similar teaching in the simpler story of the other Gospels. They tell the same tale, though without the same mystic spirit; every idea which John records is found, in embryo, somewhere in the brief, nervous, quick-moving record of the earlier writings.

In the Gospel according to St. Luke, there are recorded utterances which link together John's story and that of the others. These utterances found a resting place in the mind of the beloved disciple, and even though the language in which he records them takes a special form, even though sometimes it is difficult to decide where the Saviour's words end and his disciple's comment begins, we may readily believe that "the teaching is derived from our Lord himself, actually taught by him in the days of his flesh, and now put into permanent form, if not by the Apostle John, then by some pupil of his who stood in somewhat the same relation to him as that in which Mark stood to the Apostle Peter."

All of the evangelists are at one in their feeling of the mystery of the Lord's death, and in each we have the record, lovingly complete, of what each saw and told. What difference does it make whether they told it again and again, and others (acting as editors rather than authors) wrote what they said, or they themselves wrote with their own hands, as now seems improbable? We reach truth by instinct as well as by reason, and both reason and instinct assure us that in reading these accounts we are in the presence of assured truth.

Part of that truth is the fact of Christ's death as a sacrifice for sin. It lay at the root of all later teaching. Its appeal to the hearts of those who loved Christ made them linger over every detail of that dreadful day when he was crucified.

When Christ was crucified, the high priesthood of Israel had become a place of political patronage. Annas, the High Priest by right, was still alive; but had been deposed and retired, though the strict Jews regarded him as holding, as it were, a priesthood emeritus. Caiaphas, his son-in-law, had been named as his successor. It is said that four of the sons of Annas held the office at various times, and in view of the fact that Annas had been deposed by the Roman governor this speaks in loud words of the political astuteness of the family, if not of their corrupt connections with the civil power.

Jesus, therefore, had two ecclesiastical trials: one a formal hearing before Annas, who was probably jealous of his prestige; the other before Caiaphas, sitting as president of the Jewish Sanhedrin. Because the priestly cabal were determined upon his death, he also had a civil trial, since only the representative of the Roman government could pronounce a death sentence. Then, because Pilate the Governor found the whole affair a trying and disagreeable business and had the happy thought of patching up a political friendship with Herod, who had been at odds with him, by paying him the compliment of turning the case over to his jurisdiction, Jesus had two civil hearings; three in fact: one before Herod, two before Pilate—because it was at a second hearing that he was condemned.

Early Friday morning, after his arrest, he was taken before Annas. It was here that Peter's denial of him occurred. The disciples had all fled; but Peter and John, after a while, plucked up courage to follow the crowd. Because John was known in the High Priest's house, the young girl who acted as a servant at the porter's gate allowed both to enter the palace. The denial was as impulsive as were all Peter's acts. "Surely you are one of this man's disciples, are you not?" This innocent question of the girl caught him unawares and he blurted out a denial. Then he ran out into the courtyard and stood by the charcoal fire with the soldiers.

On the other side of the courtyard, Jesus had been brought to face Annas. Questioned as to his teaching, he pointed to the spectators and said, with dignity, "These men know what I have taught; ask them." It was a veiled rebuke, and at once some of the sycophant servants began to beat him and demand, "Is it thus you answer the High Priest?" "If I have spoken ill," he replied, "give testimony; but if I have spoken well, why smite me?" Annas was baffled and annoyed; but he had played his part and had his honors, and so sent the prisoner to Caiaphas. As they stood ready to depart, Peter felt the suspicious eyes of the soldiers on him and began with braggadocio to join in their conversation. His rough burr betrayed him and they also accused him. The girl at the gate having run in, probably, and mischievously tormented him, her taunts and their

questioning plunged him into a second denial.
It was then that one of the relatives of Malchus,
whom he had attacked in the garden, recognized
him, and with his accusation, Peter denied again,
this time with an oath. The cock-crowing had begun already, but Peter hardly noticed the first
crowing; now the sound came to his ears plainly,
and he remembered—remembered, and turned to
see Christ's eyes upon him, and throwing his cloak
over his face rushed out into the street, shaking
with sobs of penitence.

Afterward followed the hasty summoning of
the Sanhedrin and the trial before Caiaphas.
Hardly a single provision of the law was obeyed.
Witnesses gave their testimony informally and
contradicted each other. Some accused him of
declaring that he would tear down the temple.
Finally, Caiaphas, excited and impatient, put him
on oath. "Now, then, tell us under oath," he
said, "are you the Messiah?" "I am," was the
reply—and then: "Hereafter you will see the
Son of Man seated on the right hand of power
and coming in the clouds of heaven."

It was enough. With a shout of indignation,
the High Priest plucked at his clothes, denounced
the blasphemy, and called on the senate to pronounce sentence. By acclamation, not by vote
after deliberation, as the law provided, he was
condemned to death.

Condemned for what? The record is plain. Because he had claimed divine powers. Even though the words may have been capable of another interpretation, that was the ground of the judgment. And had he not said once before something of a like nature, "Before Abraham was, I am," and had they not on that occasion sought to stone him to death? He was condemned because he claimed to be the Son of God.

Because the penalty was death, the case then went to Pontius Pilate, the governor, an official already at odds with the Jews, unpopular and knowing it, anxious to vent upon them his dislikes, yet of too weak a nature to defy them in a pinch. There was much angry dispute between Pilate and the Jewish officials, and he tried to rid himself of the case, but in vain.

At last he questioned the prisoner himself. "Are you a king?" he asked. Yes, but my kingdom is not of this world. "For this end was I born, for this I came into the world, that I might testify to the truth."

"Ah," said Pilate, "what is truth?" And thinking him a harmless visionary, he declared, "I find no fault in the man."

So the trial went on: Pilate urging the prisoner to further answers and annoyed at his silence; and finally catching the word Galilean and, remembering Herod's presence in the city, sending him off to the court of the tetrarch.

Herod merely made sport of the prisoner, disappointed in his hope of seeing a miracle worker, and vented his displeasure upon him by turning him over to the bodyguard of soldiers, who mockingly arrayed him in royal garments and sent him back to Pilate.

The rest was short business—short, but cruel. Pilate tried once more to release the man, but the Jews cried out that if he did so he was likely to get into trouble with the Emperor. Again, Pilate offered to chastise him before he was released, but that was not enough. Just then the holiday crowd came rushing in, demanding the release of a prisoner, as was the custom at the festival time, and Pilate, hoping against hope, offered them their choice of Jesus or a political prisoner called Barabbas. Urged on by the priests, they were quick to choose, and Barabbas was released and Jesus was delivered to be crucified.

Not, however, before Pilate had received warning from his wife of a dream she had had about the man; not before he had gone through the futile gesture of publicly washing his hands of the whole matter; not before he had delivered him to be scourged, and the soldiers had mocked him and thrust a thorny crown on his head; not before the governor himself in one last weak appeal had brought the bleeding man before the crowd; not before he had endeavored to make the prisoner speak by reminding him of the governor's authority; not before he had, in turn, been reminded that all authority is of God.

At last the choice was given again: "Shall I crucify your king?" At last the choice was made in words that were a repudiation of all their religious beliefs, "We have no king but Cæsar." At last, wearing the crown and carrying the cross, the Saviour moved out on the sorrowful way to Calvary.

There they crucified him; two thieves with him, one on each side; with a mocking title, by Pilate's orders, nailed to his cross, "The King of the Jews."

On the way he had some small human comfort. The women of Jerusalem wept in sympathy. Like the women of today, they were accustomed to minister to the suffering; and it was their practice to give soothing drink to those about to be executed. The women, therefore, were the ones, so it seems, who offered him a drugged wine. He declined, telling them to weep, not for him, but for their children. When he fell under the weight of the cross, Simon of Cyrene was impressed by the soldiers and made to give assistance, afterward (so tradition says) becoming a believer.

At nine o'clock he was crucified, praying for his murderers as the spikes were driven into his hands and feet: "Father, forgive them; for they know not what they do." A little later the brigand, who, with the other robber, had been reviling him, turned upon his companion, reminding him that they were suffering justly. Then, won by the Saviour's brave endurance as well as touched by his prayer for the executioners, he cried, "Lord, remember me when thou comest into thy kingdom." Quick as a flash the prayer was answered: "Today shalt thou be with me in paradise."

So they hung for nearly three hours; and it was then that Jesus, seeing a gathering storm and knowing that the increasing agony would be too much for his mother to bear, sent her home with John, his closest friend, who, with some of the women of Galilee, was lingering near the cross. "Woman, behold thy son." "Son, behold thy mother."

It was noon and he had been hanging on the cross three hours, when the sky became overcast; a sirocco from the desert coming up, probably, which presaged the earthquake of which we are told later. For three more hours he hung in the darkness; then the watchers heard a loud cry of agony, "My God, my God, why hast thou forsaken me?"

Truthful records? Who can deny it? Who can imagine the invention of such a word from such a man? Who can deny the honesty of the loving hearts that recorded it, sharp as might have been their temptation to conceal it and let men forget its possible implications, its seeming show of weakness and loss of faith? The words have always been regarded as proof of Christ's complete entrance into all human experience. They are a revelation of faith, not of despair; for they are quoted from one of the psalms (the twenty-second) with which he was doubtless comforting himself during his agony—an agony which suddenly became so sharp that this one verse rose in a loud sharp cry.

The other recorded words came quickly together at the end: "I thirst"—a cry which aroused the pity of the soldiers, who reached up to his lips a sponge soaked in sour wine. Then, in a sharp cry of agony: "It is finished." And then a sentence of peaceful submission: "Father, into thy hands I commend my spirit," and he was gone.

Later, the soldiers came to break the legs of

the two dying robbers; and finding Jesus already dead, thrust the spear into his side. John, who had returned and was standing by, saw the blood and serum gush out; saw and for some reason found faith returning.

Chapter XXIII: The Victorious Issue

HE tragic end of a career to which the apostles had committed themselves, heart and soul, left them utterly stunned. They had gone through an experience surpassingly wonderful in their life with Jesus Christ, and now everything had come to a hopeless ending. They were dazed and depressed, crushed and broken, knowing not what to do nor where to turn. They had followed their Master faithfully, if falteringly, though they understood him very dimly. When his death came, they hid behind closed doors, with shaken hearts, waiting in trembling expectancy lest their own turn come next, in despair at the shattering of their hopes and with painful penitence for their own cowardice in the crisis that had removed their Master.

Then something happened which at once changed this panic-stricken company. Men who were weak, cowardly, vacillating and despondent, suddenly became strong, confident, bold and unafraid. What had happened? There is no question as to what they believed had happened. Their Master, whom they had seen tortured to death and sealed in the tomb, was alive again. The tomb was empty; the body gone. Then, in bodily form, he had appeared among them, and they were convinced that he had conquered death. We cannot understand the power with which they bore witness to the resurrection of their Lord unless we realize the dark background of discouragement against which their new faith stood so clear.

Not only did this new faith come to men in despair; it came to men who were not in the faintest degree predisposed for such an issue. One of the strongest proofs of the Easter story is the fact that it was finally accepted and passionately believed in, despite the first skepticism of the disciples. They were not a credulous people, these followers of Christ; they were plain, sturdy, hard-headed, sensible folk, of an unimaginative nature, just the sort of people who insist on facing facts. At first they all doubted the evidence of their own senses. One of them, Thomas, refused bluntly to accept the story of the others, until he had received overwhelming proof of it.

After Jesus had died upon the cross, a rich man, Joseph of Arimathea, who was among the friends of Jesus, though not of the intimate circle of his followers, came forward to offer a resting place for his deceased friend in a new-made tomb in his garden outside Jerusalem. The body was wrapped in graveclothes and placed in this tomb on Friday, after the crucifixion. The Sabbath passed, and early in the morning of the first day of the week (Sunday, as we now call it) a little group of women went out to the grave.

The tomb was a hillside sepulchre. Inside there were slabs on which the bodies of the dead would be laid. The entrance was closed by a great stone, round, like a millstone, resting in a groove in which it could be rolled aside by those who wished to enter the tomb. This stone had been sealed by official orders, on petition of the Jews. While the women were approaching the sepulchre, they debated who could roll aside for them the heavy stone. To their amazement, when they reached the tomb, they found the stone already removed, or shattered by an earthquake, and they concluded that the body had been taken away. One of them, Mary Magdalene, hurried off to tell the apostles of the discovery, while the others lingered for a time near the grave. There they had a vision of angels, who told them that Jesus was risen and charged them to go and tell his disciples.

Meanwhile, Mary had found Peter and John. They ran at full speed to see for themselves. Years afterward John told the story. A young man then, he outran Peter and coming first to the sepulchre, stooped down and peered in, but did not enter. Then Peter arrived. Impulsively he pushed forward and went in, and then excitedly called his companion. Where the corpse had been laid, they saw something which made their hearts stand still. The body had been wrapped in graveclothes before the burial, the neck and face bare, and a napkin, or turban, wrapped about the head. So the dead are prepared for burial now, in the unchanging East, and so the Lord's body was prepared. When the two apostles looked, they saw everything in perfect order; no sign of confusion, no bloodstained garments thrown aside, as if the body had been removed; nor, on the other hand, any evidence that the body, clothing and all, had been taken away by marauders; the clothes were still there, but lying flat on the slab, even the turban, still with the fold or roll in it, lying where the head had rested.

John says that "he saw and believed." What did he see? Evidently that the clothes had fallen undisturbed, lying as if the body had exhaled out of them, evanished, without deranging the wrappings. That was what brought belief to John in a flash. To find the body gone might have meant nothing, though others sought desperately for a natural explanation of its disappearance; to find signs of confusion would have indicated theft;

but to see the winding cloths dropped down of their own weight and of the weight of the spices within their folds—that indicated only one thing: that the body had risen out of them. The hand of man had no part in this work. A quick glance told them that a miracle had happened. They saw—and what they saw made belief sure. It was the beginning of reasoned conviction; a first flash of faith.

Leaving the tomb, the two disciples moved slowly back to the city, marvelling at what they had seen. Meanwhile, Mary had returned to the tomb. She stood near the entrance, weeping, and a little while later gained courage to look in. Lo! the tomb was no longer untenanted. At the head and feet, where the body had been laid, were angels, who asked why she wept. "Because they have taken away my Lord," she said, "and I know not where they have laid him." Then, turning about, she saw in the dim light another figure. Dazed and unable to collect her thoughts, her first impulse was a natural one. The gardener— of course. Perhaps he had taken away the body, not caring to have the curious folk trampling through the place when they came to look and talk. He asked the same question, "Why are you weeping? Whom are you seeking?" "Tell me," she cried, "where have you laid him?" And then she heard a familiar voice, "Mary," and looking closely recognized Jesus and fell down to clasp his feet and cry out, "Oh, my Master." "Touch me not," he commanded; "do not cling to me, for I am not yet ascended to my Father; but go to my brethren and tell them, 'I ascend unto my Father and your Father, and to my God and your God.'"

This was the first of the resurrection appearances. Now let us return to the other women. They were on their way back to the city, to find the disciples. In their agitation and alarm, they probably became separated and entered the city by different roads. One group, in their fear and astonishment, said nothing to anyone; the others, so one account says, were greeted by the vision of Christ, whom they fell down and reverenced. They came quickly to the disciples, with their excited story; but these had not yet heard of the visit of Peter and John, and the words of the women seemed to them but an idle tale. Later, Mary Magdalene came with her story of the vision of the risen Christ; but this, too, fell on dull ears. That is hardly surprising, even were Peter and John already with the others. It is just one more evidence of the truth of the story. The disciples were not in an expectant mood. They were not ready to receive news of a miracle. Their very slowness to believe adds strength to the account. They believed only under the compulsion of absolute proof.

That same afternoon two disciples were walking to the village of Emmaus, about seven or eight miles from Jerusalem. They were not apostles, but were of the larger group, the rank and file of the followers of Christ. They had heard something, however, of the strange news which was circulating in the apostolic company; but, like the others, they could not understand and they were still stunned and bewildered. St. Luke's Gospel tells their story in detail, and there is a tradition that he himself was one of the two men, Cleopas being the other.

The story of their walk is told so naturally and simply that it bears in every sentence the marks of truth. In the bewilderment of their bereavement, they talked drearily of the past, of all their hopes, of their belief in Jesus as the Messiah, of their disappointment in his mission, of the failure of his plan, and the tragic end of his life. As they were walking, a stranger joined them, whom they supposed to be one of the thousands of pilgrims who had come up to Jerusalem for the feast. He asked them why they were so sad as they walked and talked, and apparently they were a little annoyed at his ignorance. Could it be that there was anyone in Jerusalem who did not know the things that had come to pass there in the last few days? Was he some foreigner of the Dispersion, sojourning in the holy city and unaware of the thing that had made this Passover season different from every other? They began to explain about it all. It was impossible to think or talk about anything else.

Soon, however, the stranger took the lead in the conversation. Their eyes opened in wide astonishment at the things he said. Beginning with the earliest prophecies, he explained how the Messiah was a predestined sufferer and through suffering was to enter into his glory. What a conversation it must have been! We may think of him, for example, reminding them of the words in the prophecy of Isaiah: "He is despised and rejected of men; a man of sorrows and acquainted with grief. He was wounded for our transgressions; he was bruised for our iniquities; the chastisement of our peace was upon him, and with his stripes we are healed." Very quickly they threw off their lethargy and listened breathlessly. The whole tangled story suddenly became plain. Their dull despair gave way to wild hopes. New courage came into their hearts. The talk was so interesting that before they knew it they were at their own door and the stranger was saying his farewells and starting down the road. Then they aroused themselves, clung to him, begged him to come in and share their hospitality and tell them more. When, at their urging, he had entered the room, it seemed quite the natural thing that he should recline at the place of honor at table and say the simple blessing. He took the bread and blessed it and broke it—and they knew him! It was the Lord Jesus! Hardly had they recognized him, when he vanished. For a moment they looked at each other; in one breathless sentence they told each other how their hearts had strangely burned within them, as he talked with them in the way. Then they hurried out of the house and down the road and back to Jerusalem, and in a little while they were in the upper room, to tell of the Christ who had died and was alive again. There they found the apostles with their own excited story of other appearances; and while they were yet speaking, the Master came again.

He came suddenly and in a strange way. They seem all to have been talking—as doubtless they would, in their excitement, when a hush fell on them. Jesus was present! The doors were closed, and there had been no knock, nor had anyone seen him enter; yet there he stood. As he moved toward them, he said, "Peace be unto you." They were frightened beyond words, thinking they saw a specter; but he showed them his hands and his wounded side and then renewed their apostolic commission: "As the Father has sent me, even so send I you"; and he breathed on them, and said: "Receive the Holy Spirit. Whosoever sins you remit, they are remitted unto them, and whosoever sins you retain, they are retained."

Thomas was not with the others at this appearance of the Lord; and when informed of it, refused to believe. "Unless I see in his hands the print of the nails, and put my finger into the print of the nails, and put my hand into his side," he said, "I will in no wise believe it." A week later his test was met. They were again in the room, with closed doors, and this time Thomas had joined the company. Again a hush and again the realization that Jesus was present. "Reach here your finger," he said to Thomas, "and see my hands; and reach here your hand and put it into my side, and be not faithless, but believing." And Thomas fell on his knees at the Master's feet, with his cry of faith, "My Lord and my God."

This record seems originally to have closed St. John's Gospel, but as an afterthought he adds one other incident, very personal, of an appearance of the Master on the seashore. Seven of the apostles were in the boat fishing, when he appeared and learning that they had caught nothing, ordered them to cast the net on the right side. They obeyed, and the net was hauled up so filled that they could not draw it. Again there is John's flashing faith. "It is the Lord," he cried, and Peter plunged into the water to swim to shore, the others following in the boat. There they saw preparation made for their morning meal.

Afterward the three—Jesus, Peter and John— walked along the shore. "Simon, son of Jonas," the Master asked, "have you fuller regard and affection for me than for these?" "Yes, Lord," said Simon, "you know how passionately I love you." "Then feed my lambs." Again: "Simon, are you sure of your regard for me?" "Oh, Master, you know I love you passionately." "Tend my sheep." Again: "Simon, are you sure even of your passionate devotion?" And Peter, grieved, said: "Lord, you know all things, you surely see how devotedly I love you." "Feed my sheep."

And then, almost immediately, seeing John who had fallen behind them, Peter asked what this man was to do. "If I will that he should tarry until I come again, what business is that of yours?" said Jesus. "Do you but see to it that you follow me."

There are records of other risen appearances, none of them told in such detail. He was seen by Peter and James singly, was seen by some in groups, was seen by hundreds of others together. There are special difficulties about the resurrection narratives. The authentic text of St. Mark's Gospel, for example, ends abruptly and the story of the resurrection is a hasty and incomplete summary. St. Matthew's Gospel is hardly more satisfactory, especially in its connecting the resurrection with the earthquake which seems to have followed upon the crucifixion. How it came about that the records are so meager we do not know; but there can be little question as to the actual belief of the apostles. There must have been a record, now lost, which would have concluded St. Mark; for there we have recorded the assurance of Christ to his disciples at the Last Supper, "After I am raised up, I will go before you into Galilee." And the change in Peter himself is beyond question. He *was* turned again by the Risen Christ; he *did* strengthen his brethren.

Nor can we escape the witness of St. Paul, who declares that he received his knowledge of the facts from "the Twelve" and wrote at an early date. The historical fact is that Christ appeared again and again to his disciples, even though we may be uncertain as to the form or order of his appearances.

The disciples had been with him and had known him so long in the flesh, that they had to be prepared in this way for the time of his departure.

The resurrection appearances slowly taught them that he was always with them. One moment they were alone in the upper room, the next he came and stood in their midst. They were fishing on the lake, and looked up to see him on the shore. He joined the two disciples on the way to Emmaus and vanished as soon as they recognized him. They must have met each other every morning, these disciples, with the unspoken question on their lips, "I wonder whether we shall see him today," until at length, when they had learned that he was always near, whether they saw him or not, he led them out toward Bethany and, while he was talking with them and blessing them, a cloud received him out of their sight. He had "ascended." But he had not gone away; he was present, but present after another mode; it was now a "veiled presence."

There are difficulties, of course, in explaining the details of the resurrection story. That is only natural. In any story, there would be the same difficulties. Eyewitnesses tell only what they themselves see, and it is sometimes hard to reconcile their stories, though we know beyond peradventure that each is truthful. But if there is anything on earth beyond controversy, it is that the disciples of Christ believed with all their hearts that he had risen and was alive again. Nor was their faith merely a strong belief that his life was continued in the spiritual realm. They believed that he had miraculously conquered death and that his body had not "seen corruption." It would have been easy to disabuse their minds of this belief, had his body still been in the tomb. But the grave was empty! He had been "crucified, dead and buried." Where was the body? It was gone. Where? No answer has ever been given that satisfies the reason, except the answer the apostles themselves gave.

It is an adventure into the absurd to study other theories that try to account for the apostles' faith. The explanations are so ingenious that they are more difficult to accept than the facts they seek to explain. Indeed, they are often more difficult even to state, much less defend. Some of these explanations make the disciples deceivers, who had themselves stolen the body. Some even make Christ himself a fountainhead of dishonesty, by declaring that he had not actually died, but had swooned and was resuscitated in the cooler air of the sepulchre. If that had been true, he must have acquiesced in the misunderstanding of his disciples. Thus the explanation goes again on its way, without any effort at explaining what became of the broken body in later days.

It is not surprising to find modern skeptics discarding these ancient devices for doing away with the resurrection story. They now content themselves with a denial of the actual bodily resurrection, substituting theories of a purely spiritual phenomenon which, in the last analysis, present greater difficulties than the Gospel narratives themselves.

It is not a part of our task to show what the resurrection was, nor what changes had occurred in the Lord's physical body, nor what our own spiritual bodies may be, nor to what the resurrection world may be likened. These are matters beyond human experience and impossible of explanation, therefore, in human language. Certainly, it is not our task to defend outworn theories about the bodily resurrection which defy ascertained facts. The disciples saw Jesus in a state of transition or change, on the boundary of two worlds, the physical and the spiritual. He had his own body and showed them the marks of identification, but it was a body that could pass through closed doors and come and go at will. This is all mysterious, and the mystery cannot be explained. We are merely concerned to show that anything less than the actual miraculous resurrection of Christ, and his real appearance among his disciples, cannot explain what happened as the victorious issue of the cross.

It is utterly impossible to conceive of such a

belief as that which the apostles unquestionably held arising, spreading widely, becoming accepted beyond doubt and being made the foundation of the Christian Church—utterly impossible to conceive of this on any other hypothesis than the reality of the fact itself. Only this can explain the change in the disciples themselves, the work they accomplished, and the church they established. Ghosts and visions are not seen by crowds of people together. Great institutions are not built out of the fabric of dreams. Men are not changed, as the disciples were changed, by self-deception, enthusiasm, or the hysteria of an over-wrought, high-strung and intensely emotional woman. Weak men do not defy authority, face death, convert thousands to their beliefs, reverse the entire course of their lives, and revolutionize the world, unless there is a sufficient cause to account for the fact that out of weakness they have been made strong. The story of Christ's triumph and of their renewal in the power of his resurrection is the only adequate explanation of the work of the apostles and of the spiritual movement which had its impetus from them. Nothing but a determined refusal to accept the supernatural could, in the face of all this, allow persistent rejection of the Lord's resurrection.

Something changed the old Sabbath into the new Sunday and that something was the Easter victory. Something made the Holy Communion more than the memory of a dead friend. Something other than credulous expectancy lifted the apostles out of despair and set them to the establishment of a church which, with all its failures and all its weakness and error, has always borne witness to the Lord in whom it still believes.

In these days, people approach the supernatural very gingerly. We try to ignore it and leave it and "pass it by on the other side." It cannot be done. We make nothing of Christianity, if we leave out the supernatural. Without it, there would be no gospel. Only when we accept Christ as the Risen Lord and see in his triumph a new creative act, do we come to the gospel the apostles preached. That sent them out conquering and to conquer, attempting a seemingly impossible task with undying courage. It "drove them out into the world like thunderbolts." It has made Christianity "good news," not "good advice."

Chapter XXIV: His Tremendous Claims

WHEN Jesus Christ died upon the cross, no one, not even his apostles, knew that he was the incarnate Son of God. Even after he had risen from the dead, no one at first clearly understood. The whole idea of an Incarnation—God manifesting Himself in the flesh—is so stupendous that it could not quickly be grasped, even by those who were closest to Jesus Christ during his life. How could they have been expected to accept such an interpretation of his life? Had they guessed it, how could they have maintained their fellowship with him? That intimacy of companionship was necessary, if they were to absorb his teaching and be molded to his purpose. Suppose they had, from the start, known fully who he was, their relations with him would have lost the freedom of friendly intercourse. Even when they had reached a point in their intercourse where they had practically put him in the place of God in their hearts, they were not conscious of what their attitude toward him meant. Only as instinctive worship passed into reasoned belief did their faith find clear expression.

Even after the resurrection they were slow to grasp the meaning of his victory—how could it have been otherwise? For forty days Jesus still companied with them, before "he was taken up, and a cloud received him out of their sight." We are told that during these days he taught them more fully of "the things pertaining to the Kingdom of God." We find them immediately after his ascension establishing a church, choosing a successor to Judas as one of their number, waiting for the coming of the Holy Spirit, and then, when the Pentecostal gift had been received, going out to preach Christ and the power of his resurrection. Evidently, also, they had received definite instruction from their Master about the organization and work of the church, for they were steadfast in "doctrine," in "fellowship," in "the breaking of the bread," in "the prayers"—in other words, they had a body of definite teaching, an organization, set forms of devotion, and the regular celebration of the Holy Communion.

And they preached Christ—preached him with such power that Peter's first sermon on the Day of Pentecost brought three thousand persons to the new faith. Yet when we read the report of the sermon we find its creed somewhat *naïve* as compared with later teaching. He speaks of "Jesus of Nazareth, a man approved of God among you by miracles and wonders and signs. . . This Jesus has God raised up, whereof we all are witnesses . . . God has made this same Jesus, whom you crucified, both Lord and Christ. . . Repent, and be baptized every one of you in the name of Jesus Christ for the remission of sins, and you shall receive the gift of the Holy Spirit." The whole tone of the address is unlike the later preaching of Paul, for example, and quite different in its method of approach from the way in which John sets forth the faith.

From this, it has been argued that the later faith was a development—an unwarranted change from the simple, undogmatic belief of the early days. A development it was, but merely in the sense that it was the result of steady thinking—the effort to give expression to a faith which the apostles had already proclaimed by their actions. From the beginning they had done all "in the name of the Lord Jesus"; he was "the Prince of Life"; "the Son of God, Jesus, whom God sent to bless you." They prayed not only "in the name of the Lord Jesus," but to Jesus himself. Stephen, the first martyr, "saw the glory of God, and Jesus standing on the right hand of God," and died crying, "Lord Jesus, receive my spirit."

Eventually the time came when it was impossible to continue to act toward Jesus as God without asking why. They had been brought by an irresistible impulse to worship their Master, but religious emotions cannot continue indefinitely without a logical basis. Men are compelled to ask questions; they want to know "the reason of things." Meanwhile, too, the apostles were in a special way under the guidance of the Holy Spirit, whom Jesus had promised to send, to "guide them into all truth," to "teach them all things," and to "bring all things to their remembrance" that he had said unto them.

The Gospel according to St. John is written in the light of this fuller remembrance, but its interpretation of the life of Jesus Christ is not essentially different from the underlying doctrine of the earlier Gospels. In them, also, we see a great and wonderful life, which leads the disciples on and on, and yet ever extends beyond their understanding. As yet they had no theory about Christ; they felt his divine greatness.

Stop to consider the picture they paint. It is a picture of a little group of men following their Master with ever-increasing amazement. They see one who is human like themselves, bound by the strictest human limitations, subject to human infirmities; yet one the mystery of whose person they can never escape. He seems anxious that they should consider this mystery. "Who do men say that I, the Son of Man, am?" "Who do you say that I am?" What an astonishing thing that the question should be asked! One cannot explain it wholly on the supposition that Jesus wished to clarify their thoughts about the office of the expected Messiah.

What an astonishing thing that the question should still be asked! What other world leader ever concentrated thought in this way on his own person? What other religion stands or falls by the answer to such a question? What other teacher makes the question so insistent that it compels serious thought in all future centuries?

Now that the Gospel according to St. Mark is recognized as the earliest of our written Gospels, some extraordinary considerations are thrust upon us. For example, it is the Gospel of Christ's "wonderful works": how can these records ever be wrested out of the Gospel, if this primitive narrative lays such emphasis on them? They are no later accretions. How can they be explained as the works of a purely human Christ?

While the earlier Gospels unconsciously show how little the disciples were able to understand, they leave no doubt as to the greatness of the Figure they were called upon to understand. Jesus heals the sick, raises the dead, has authority over the powers of nature. He is the Son of Man, who asks men to forsake father and mother, wife and children, rather than to fail to follow him. A man who excused himself from immediate discipleship, that he might attend his father's declining years, is told to "let the dead bury their dead." Another who would first go and bid farewell to his family is warned against putting his hand to the plough, only to turn back. Those who follow must deny themselves and take up the cross with Jesus.

He is the Son of Man who teaches with such authority that though heaven and earth shall pass away, his words will never pass away. All things have been delivered to him by the Father. No man knows the Father, but he to whom the Son will reveal Him. He revises the God-given law. He is Lord of the Sabbath. He will give his life "a ransom for many." He comes "to seek and to save." He concentrates all the mystery of his divine consciousness in a sacramental act, and gives his body and blood as the food of the soul. He "goes as it is written of him," but goes willingly as one whose blood is "shed for many for the remission of sins." He calls to himself all who labor and are heavy laden and promises to give them rest. He "has power on earth to forgive sins." He will "rise again the third day." He will come again "in clouds, with great power and glory." He will be seen then "sitting on the right hand of power." His "fan is in his hand," as he comes in judgment. He is "the Christ, the Son of the Blessed."

Most startling of all, of course, is his claim to be the judge of men. "The Father judges no man by Himself. He gives over all judgment to the Son." He gives him this authority to pronounce judgment, "because he is the Son of Man," tempted as we are and touched with the feeling of our infirmities; but the Son is given authority also, that "all men may honor me as they honor the Father."

These last words are found in St. John, but St. Mark's primitive Gospel makes it plain that Jesus is to come again in glory to judge the world, and St. Matthew's Gospel gives the grounds on which the judgment will be based:

"The Son of Man shall come in glory, and all the holy angels with him . . . . . Then shall he sit upon the throne of his glory . . . . . Then shall the King say unto them on his right hand, Come, ye blessed of my Father, inherit the kingdom prepared for you from the beginning of the world. For I was an hungered, and ye gave me meat; I was thirsty and ye gave me drink; I was a stranger, and ye took me in; naked, and ye clothed me; I was sick, and ye visited me; I was in prison, and ye came unto me.

"Then shall the righteous answer him, saying, Lord, when saw we thee an hungered, and

fed thee? or thirsty, and gave thee drink?
When saw we thee a stranger, and took thee
in? or naked, and clothed thee? Or when saw
we thee sick, or in prison, and came unto thee?

"And the King shall answer and say unto
them, Verily, I say unto you, Inasmuch as ye
have done it unto one of the least of these my
brethren, ye have done it unto me."

Surely, there is no difference between the Lord
of whom the earlier Gospels tell us, and the Lord
of whom the Apostle Paul speaks, or the Lord of
whom the Apostle John writes. Everywhere he
is seen as doing marvelous works, acting with
power, speaking with authority, entering upon a
work in full assurance that his authority is of
heaven, conscious that his death will be a blessing,
sure that it will issue in a victorious resurrection,
declaring as he vanishes from their sight that his
presence will be with them to the end of time,
always human and yet never anything but divine.

And never anything but sinless. This appears
throughout, and is a challenge Christ himself is
represented as issuing in one of his controversies
with the Pharisees. "Which of you convicteth
me of sin?" he asked them. The words suggest,
though they do not prove, his sinlessness; but the
picture of him everywhere presented shows him as
he is spoken of in one of the epistles, "holy, harm-

less, undefiled, separate from sinners"—the only good man who ever lived without consciousness of guilt. "He did no sin, neither was guile found in his mouth" are the words applied to him by one of his apostles, who could never have made the comparison had not the disciples' knowledge of his character made it easy and natural.

In the Gospel according to St. John we have the reasoned conviction of the apostles. The style and method differ to a marked degree from the language of the other Gospels, but this Gospel shows the same character in a different environment. It is the record of the Lord's ministry in Judea; and there, in constant conflict with the Pharisees, he would naturally be seen in a different light from that of the Galilean days. The Gospel was written much later, and there had been opportunity to think back over the story after the experience of later days. It was written with the distinct purpose of showing how the apostles reached their riper faith. Its record need not seem incongruous, if we remember that the Holy Spirit had recalled to the minds of Christ's followers many things which they had not understood in the days of his ministry. With this Gospel before us, as well as the other three, let us draw the portrait of Christ again. Put it in a somewhat crude way. Suppose a preacher today were to stand before his congregation and announce a message something like this:

"You need God, and you cannot come to Him but through me. You have been drawn away into sin, and I am come to seek and to save you. You want to know what God is like; those who have seen me have seen God. I call you to follow me. No rival claim, however strong, no natural affection, however deep, must interpose between you and myself. You must not love father, mother, husband, wife, or child as you love me.

"I have come to help you, because you so sadly need help. You are like silly sheep gone astray, sick, weary, torn, distracted, beaten, and driven back. I am the Good Shepherd, going out to rescue everyone who has wandered away in sin. I am without sin myself. I am from above, you are from beneath. You must honor me, as you honor God. I am the Way, the Truth, the Life; no man, I repeat, can come to God but through me. I am the light of this dark world; walk in my light. I and my Father are one; in me you see Him. No man can know God but those to whom I reveal Him.

"I have come to bring you good news of God. Some day I shall come back to see what you have done with my teaching. God has committed all judgment to me, that you may honor me as you honor Him. I know you, your past and present, your inherited traits, your special temptations, your spiritual struggles, your real motives. I know you as God knows you.

"When I come to judge you, I will read your lives like an open book, and will separate you, the good from the bad. Some of you will be banished from my presence—and from God's. Some of you I shall call before me to bless and reward. I shall judge you according to your deeds. You will know in that day for what you are condemned and for what you receive a blessing, as I recall to your minds what you have done or left undone in the service of others.

"I care for you with a pastor's heart; care for you so much that I shall soon die for you. Do not reject me or my words. Come unto me, all who are heavy laden, and I will give you rest.

"Some day you will see all this as you cannot see it now, and if you have been faithful there will be a place for you in the home of God. In His house are many mansions; if it were not so, I would have told you.

"And now I go away, to prepare a place for you. You will see me no more, till I come again to receive you to myself, though I shall always be with you, unseen. Remember me always. My body is broken and my blood shed for you. Meet me now at our last meal together, and always do what I do now, and remember that you must eat and drink of my body and blood, or there is no life in you. In me is life eternal, a very well of water for the refreshment of your souls. Remember. For I have come that you may have life, and that you may have it abundantly."

Imagine a man speaking in such language! Sometimes we are told that it is enough to follow Christ without trying to explain him. He is the best man the world ever knew! And yet these were the things he said, again and again, to his followers. Any man who said such things now would be put in custody as insane, arrested as a dangerous fanatic, or condemned as an impostor using his personal magnetism to arouse enthusiasm for himself and to excite the devotion of his followers for his own base purposes.

Again, these are exactly the things Jesus Christ said. He deliberately trained his disciples to trust him utterly. He deliberately put himself in the place of God in their hearts. That is the most offensive presumption, the worst of all possible sins, unless he were all that he claimed to be. The human glory of Jesus Christ is gone, if we try to consider it apart from his divine claims. There was an ancient dilemma, "Either Christ is God, or he is not a good man." It is true. If Christ is the best man the world has ever seen, the one man in whom all virtues have been combined and from whom sin has been eliminated, then he must be divine. Otherwise his speech is the quintessence of arrogant religious charlatanism; if he is not divine, he is not good.

The marvel is, that no one dreams of calling Jesus an impostor. Some, it is true, have made him a fiery enthusiast; some, a fanatic expecting the end of all things; some, an unworldly idealist with intuitive faith in a heavenly Father. But, like the accusers at his trial, these witnesses do not "agree together." Each omits what is inconsistent with his own theory. One after another, their portraits are discarded. None shows the many-sided character of Christ. The world has never been able to escape the mystery of his person. He has never been satisfactorily explained in terms of humanity. "Do not speak like that," Charles Lamb is reported to have said, when some one had spoken flippantly of Jesus; "do not speak like that. If Shakespeare came into this room, we should all spring to our feet; but if Jesus Christ came, we should fall on our knees."

The perpetual miracle is that we find in Jesus

everything he claimed for himself. The miracle is even greater: we find the God of Jesus in the life of Jesus. He is himself all that he said he was, and all that he declared God to be. If we were to think long and carefully of all we wish to find in God, and then describe all the hungry heart desires, the description could hardly be other than what Jesus Christ was in his earthly life. We believe in God the Father Almighty, and in Jesus Christ, his Only Son, our Lord.

Chapter XXV: A Faith to Live By

HAT difference does it make? Suppose Jesus Christ were not the Unique Son of God, would there not still be his wonderful teaching and still his life as our inspiring example? What difference does it make? Is not the essential thing to try to follow Christ, rather than to be able to define him?

The strongest believer in the deity of Christ should be the first to acknowledge the element of truth embodied in such questions. Too often, in the past, the central doctrine of Christianity has been taught in a hard, dogmatic spirit, as if it were simply a "shibboleth," or test word, by which to shut out all who cannot frame to pronounce it aright. A great many people resent what they call dogma, without having very clear ideas as to what dogma is. They are prejudiced by a not uncommon experience: doctrine has been presented to them in concentrated tabloid form, as pestilent spiritual pellets thrust upon unwilling patients. Doctrine is thus divorced from life. Whereas actually the doctrines of Chris-

[259]

tianity are the logical exponents of its facts, brief statements of truth as a basis for right living.

We needed the truth of Christ's real humanity. We needed the reminder that Christianity means trying to be like Christ. It must never be regarded merely as a system of belief; it is a way of life. Those who accepted it walked "in the way." In their preaching, the apostles showed men "the way of salvation." When Saul, unconverted and breathing out threatenings against the disciples of the Lord, went to Damascus on his errand of persecution, he went to see if he could find "any of this way." Following his conversion, he taught "after the way" which the strict Jews denounced as heresy. Two of his earliest converts met one whose knowledge was imperfect, and "expounded unto him the way of God more perfectly." When Jesus Christ would sum up in one sentence his unique relation with God and men, he said, "I am the Way, the Truth, and the Life." He summoned his followers to walk "in the ways of God." Christianity was a new plan for right living, a new way of life.

It has rightly been said that "the greatest of all heresies is a moral heresy," wherein men proclaim their belief in Christ as God, but do not treat him as God. He came declaring that certain things are important and other things are not, that some things we must never do (God being what He is) and other things we must always do, and do without reckoning the reward. He came declaring that God is our Father. He himself lived in the freedom and power of one who had committed his whole life to God in filial obedience. He asked us to show the same faith as "children of our Father which is in heaven," striving to be perfect, "even as the Father in heaven is perfect." If he is God, he must be treated as God; his teaching cannot be ignored. The real heresy is the practical denial of Christ made by those who are unwilling to take him at his word. The real opposition to the Gospel is the skepticism which acts on the quiet assumption that Christ's plan of life will not work in a rough world like ours; that while it is academically sound and idealistically beautiful, it has been smashed to pieces by the hard facts of life, and cannot be acted upon without reservations and exceptions.

We need, then, to be pulled up with a sharp reminder that any declaration of Christ's divinity made with our lips must prove itself in our lives. Christianity was, first of all, the Way, and we must walk in it. Of late the world has been suspecting that perhaps, after all, Christ's plan was right. After long ignoring him, we find that in turning from his way of life we have been marching straight to disaster. The old plan of life has broken down, and men are looking wistfully to Christ's way. At last, we are beginning to see that it may really be wisest to put "first things first" and seek God's Kingdom and His righteousness before all else. Economists and statesmen are beginning to talk in strange ways of taking Christ's spirit even into national and international relations. They have begun to dread the social and economic upheaval which is sure to issue out of complete disregard of Christ and Christian brotherhood.

Yet we shall never find men accepting Christ's way if they regard him only as human. It is one thing to have wonderful and beautiful teaching, but it is another thing to have this teaching come with the authority of God. How else can we be sure that Christ is not a dreamer whose dreams will never come true? Unless we are under the conviction that when he speaks his voice is the voice of God, there can be no compulsion to accept his leadership. His own attempt to live a filial life with God his Father ended at Calvary. If his cross is but the world's worst tragedy, instead of God's adventure for the race, then the springs of hope are dried up forever. What does he know of God more than the rest of mankind, save as high thoughts of God will always be held by men whose own lives are high and fine? "The best God is the God of the best men. An honest God's the noblest work of man." Here we have a noble man creating God in his own image, but how can we be sure that he knew? If those who have seen him have not seen the Father, then nobody knows what God is like and nobody ever will know. If Christ's proffered forgiveness and help do not come by God's authority, we have heard but a swan song of gracious kindliness from a visionary lover of mankind. As a plain matter of fact, is it not true that, so far as men could see, the God of Jesus Christ failed him at the last? This faith of his could not stand the strain of contact with the sharp actualities of life. He tried out his theory, and it proved to be a mistake, however glorious a mistake; it was a dream, a dream of beauty and splendor, but only a dream, nevertheless.

That is the inevitable conclusion to which one is driven who leaves the divine out of consideration in the attempt to understand Jesus Christ. Apart from belief that he "spoke that which he knew" and "testified to that which he had seen," his life seems built upon a tragic blunder. Only as we believe that the voice which speaks is the voice of God, can we accept his view and seek to follow him. Only as we see his ultimate triumph in the resurrection, which "declared him to be the Son of God with power," does the finality and completeness of his plan of life become clear.

The first proclamation of the Gospel was concerned almost entirely with this thought of the resurrection as a great victory for Christ, which proved his authority and vindicated his claims. The disciples had been cast into the lowest depths by the tragedy of Calvary, and it was natural, therefore, that the resurrection should appeal to them first in this way. It meant that Christ had conquered; it meant that he had been proved right; it meant that every claim he had made for himself and everything he had said about God had been put to the supreme test and had come out of the fire triumphant. Their one thought was to blaze abroad the news that their Master had risen from death and failure and was passing to the glory of the Father. They were possessed by this idea of the glorified Christ, whom God had exalted. He was right—a thousand times he was right. His resurrection gloriously proved it.

Afterward they saw other aspects of the truth. To St. Paul, more than anyone else, we owe the practical application of the truths of the gospel to human needs, though of course, the same teaching is found in the earliest acts of the apostles in less formal ways. The first fresh teaching carried the fact of the resurrection down from

Christ's throne of triumph to man's need. If Jesus became man, lived as man, died as man, and as man rose again, his experience must be typical. A risen and triumphant Christ is a pledge of a risen humanity. And a risen and triumphant humanity is the proof that in seeking to save our life we lose it, and in losing life for Christ's sake we gain a greater life. Without the hope of immortality, much of the teaching of Jesus falls to the ground. His firm and implicit faith in the goodness of God issued in triumph for himself. There must be the same hope and expectation for us, if we are to hold fast the same faith.

There is, in most men, a deep and passionate yearning to know what lies beyond this earthly life. The apostles were sure of their Lord's triumph over death; they were just as sure that his resurrection was a pledge of their own. Therein, again, lay the wonder of their message. The empty tomb meant the opening of the gate of death for all.

Jesus himself never argued about a future life —argument is a terrible trifling for human hearts sick with their sense of loss. He did not explain difficulties—how could they be explained, when there is no language of human experience in which to phrase the explanation? He did not give details—when all is said, of what importance are details about the future life, by comparison with the great fact itself?

Jesus simply took for granted that death is a mere turn on the road to life eternal, because God being what He is, and man being God's child, it could not be otherwise. He filled men's hearts with trust in the Heavenly Father; he made them understand the real value of human life; he made belief in immortality rest upon God's moral character. The man who would have his hope in immortality pass into certainty must start with full recognition of this teaching of Jesus.

But there again: how does he know that the teaching is true, unless Christ speaks as one who brings a message from Heaven? We cannot be satisfied with the statements of a teacher who by instinct, intuition, observation, or idealism infers that God is Father; he must be one who declares a truth of which he has positive knowledge. It was said of Thomas Carlyle that once he passed a wayside crucifix in Brittany, and standing before it, said, "Aye, poor fellow, your day's up now." Time passed and the sorrow of his life came in the death of his wife. Some one read to him, an old man in the chill and shadow of the approaching night, the familiar words, "Let not your heart be troubled. Believe in God; believe also in me. In my Father's house are many mansions; if it were not so, I would have told you. I go to prepare a place for you." And Carlyle cried out, "Aye, if you were God, you had a right to say that, but if you were only a man, what do you know more than the rest of us?"

We believe in immortality, because we have it on the authority of one "who had a right" to tell us of it. The resurrection of Christ made assurance doubly sure. All that he taught of immortality was confirmed when he himself was shown to be alive. It was this, next, that the apostles proclaimed with triumphant boldness, with a challenge clear, sharp, direct, decisive.

One more thing the first teachers of Christianity made clear: that the death on Calvary was more than an ordinary death and that it has power of forgiveness and renewal for men. There, again, there is more in the picture than a human Christ fulfils. Not that we should ever forget how human he was, how completely human, with humanity's limitations. His life, when we remember that, has a haunting beauty; it casts a spell upon the mind; it stills the soul. It makes us see Christ, as we never saw him before, in relation to the world's life and the world's need. We find in his example inspiration that had been almost lost. The thought of his cross is very moving, as the greatest act of heroism and self-sacrifice in history.

But that is not enough, nor does such a human sacrifice explain all the mysterious words Christ himself said about his death. It does not explain all his premonitions and warnings. It does not explain the memorial he instituted after the Last Supper. It does not explain what he said about giving his life a ransom for many. It does not explain how, as the Good Shepherd, he lays down his life for the sheep. It is a very poor reflection of the glowing anticipations of the last of the prophets, who called him "the Lamb of God that takes away the sin of the world." No, Jesus is Saviour as well as Master. A great scientist has said that "at the foot of the cross men have a perennial experience of relief and renovation."

Sin is more than an unfortunate slip, a foolish mistake, or a grave misfortune. It is the deliberate setting of the human will against the will of God. There is need of some unmistakable disclosure of the heart of God before we can see this. Such a revelation we have in the cross of Christ. Just as any serious attempt to measure our lives over against the life of Jesus Christ convinces us that he is a direct gift of God, so, too, any such comparison forces upon us a sense of the awfulness of sin and the need of deliverance. Just as human forgiveness, at its best, is saved from being demoralizing when, for example, the forgiven child is made to see the pain its fault has brought to the forgiving parent; so the cross of Christ makes us see the shame and the pain of sin, when divine forgiveness comes freely, but comes by divine love bearing with us our sins or their results.

All of this we cannot see if Calvary is but one of the greatest tragedies of history. We must see the cross as evidence of the eternal purpose of the Father, who will never use force to restrain and compel, but conquers by the power of love. If God's purpose is to create a human family, for such a purpose force is not power, it is weakness. God is almighty, but His might is the power of affection only. That was His method in the sacrifice of Calvary, and it has always been His method: Christ was the Lamb slain from the foundation of the world. If Jesus really rose, we have proof that love is almighty, and in the end will win. If he really is the Son of God, we have the message from God Himself, even though love be still despised and rejected of men.

If God is not the God whom Jesus Christ revealed, He ought to be. We can never, now, be satisfied with any other. Were we to catalogue all the qualities we desire in God, we should find them all in the God of Jesus—and much more besides. All we can ever ask for, Christianity had all the while to give. And Jesus himself is the nearest to God we have ever known or heard of;

we cannot dream of a Deity other or better than Christ.

There are two great difficulties in matters of faith which stand out as the peculiar problems of today. The first is, the increasing difficulty of believing in God as a loving Father. The second is, a clear recognition of the fact that unless we can so believe in God as Father, we cannot believe in Him at all. The world is more sensitive to the problem of evil than it has ever been before. We have learned so much of the apparent heartlessness of the universe that a faith which can survive the test of serious thought makes real demands upon us. George Tyrell once said that: "To believe that this terrible machine world of ours is really from God, in God, and unto God, and that through it, and in spite of its blind fatality, all things work together for good —that is faith in long trousers! All other is faith in knickerbockers!"

Faith in long trousers! A man's faith, rugged and sure, despite the hard knocks it has received since the days when he thought only as a child and understood only as a child. Never have men realized as they do now the problem of human suffering and sorrow; never have they felt so keenly the waste of life. Other generations saw the heartlessness of nature, red in tooth and claw, which shrieks out against belief in a loving God.

We have passed through worse tragedy. During and since the Great War all the multiplied doubts that ever troubled men's souls have increased a hundredfold. And this has made us painfully aware, also, of other evils, needless cruelties, social injustice and disorder, glaring inequalities— all making the idea of a God of Love the most difficult of all doctrines.

And yet it must be a God of Love, or we cannot believe in any God. Does it occur to us to ask, why? The answer is sure and certain. Because the conception of God which Jesus taught has gradually taken hold of men. It was a long time before the world began to appreciate his teaching, but at last it has so seized upon our hearts and consciences that we can never be satisfied with any kind of God except the God in whom Jesus believed. The very difficulties which most oppress us spring out of his teaching—and out of the new standards of human life, also, which he gave; standards which have lifted our thoughts high enough to make us sensitive to all that appears to contradict and destroy faith in God's goodness and the possibilities of good in His children.

Is it too much to say, then, that there is no stopping place between faith in Christ's deity and blank agnosticism? There can hardly be a doubt in the minds of thinking men that the chief cause of the moral laxity of modern life runs back into indefiniteness of faith. In general, the way we behave depends upon our attitude toward spiritual verities. If we have no definite ideas as to the meaning and purpose of life, moral standards are bound to fall. If we have no certainty about God, we are not likely to be burdened with the effort to please Him. If there can be found no real authority in the teaching of Christ, it will have loose hold upon us.

But if Jesus was what he claimed to be, and what his disciples believed him to be, then everything that he was, God is; all that he said, God still says; all that he did, God still does; all that he felt, God feels. The real question is: Have we, or have we not, an authoritative revelation of God in Jesus Christ? If we have such a revelation, then religion becomes fresh, real, wonderful. God becomes near, friendly, approachable. Service becomes the glad labor of those who are fellow workers with God. Worship becomes devotion to a Person whom we know and have seen.

God is like Christ. That is the essence of Christianity. It is not enough to say that Christ is Godlike; no, God is Christlike. "The heart of God is as the heart of Jesus." That is our standing ground amid all the changes of time, though all things on earth shout denial. It remains our constant belief, though wars ravage the earth and social injustice ruin the oppressed, and sickness and sorrow break human hearts. We shall never understand the problem of evil. Without the Son of God, we are in blank despair. With Jesus as Lord and God, we can trust, even though we do not understand.

God is like Christ. It is what Christ himself said when he declared that those who had seen him had seen the Father. It is what St. Paul meant when he spoke of the light of the knowledge of the glory of God in the face of Jesus Christ. It is what St. John meant when he declared, with breathless devotion, that in their intercourse with Jesus the apostles had actually seen and heard, their eyes had gazed upon, and their hands had handled the Word of Life.